CHURCH
MUSIC

CHURCH MUSIC

Practical Methods in Building a Successful Music Program. . .

By Lindsay Terry

SWORD of the LORD
PUBLISHERS
P.O. BOX 1099, MURFREESBORO, TN 37133

ISBN 0-87398-128-6

Printed and bound in the United States of America.

Table of Contents

INTRODUCTION

Lindsay Terry has invested many years in the field of sacred music. He has worked with some of the outstanding preachers in America. He has developed and directed outstanding church music programs.

With such a background he is eminently qualified to author this book that sets forth practical methods for building a successful music program. He has written out of his own rich experience and has shared the acquired knowledge that has come out of that experience.

I recommend this volume to all who are interested in the ministry of church music.

John W. Peterson

PREFACE

One of the great needs in Christianity today is for our churches to have more effective music programs. In writing this book I have tried to pull from more than twenty years of experience in several churches, large and small, to pass along some methods and procedures that have proven effective and successful.

This volume is intended for the layman as well as the minister of music. There are instructions that every church member should read in order to have a greater understanding of the needs and the goals of the music program of his church.

Music is very near to the heart of God. He has a great deal to say about it in the Bible, as you will see in Chapter One. He has set down certain instructions concerning our daily lives, which include our music.

A major portion of the music program of any church is the organization and the administration of the various choirs and special groups. I have tried to help in this area, especially.

No music director or choir member will be worth a hill of beans to his congregation unless he buries, deep in his breast, a philosophy of accomplishment at any cost. I have given some instruction in this area, also.

Take these ideas and suggestions—change them if it helps—and build, for the glory of God, a music program that will have life and joy.

Lindsay L. Terry

1979

FOREWORD

There is no great New Testament church that is not a singing church. When I wrote the books, *The Ten Largest Sunday Schools* and *America's Fastest Growing Churches,* I noted that their music was different from the typical American church. I heard Lindsay Terry say, "Church music comes from Bible doctrine." I knew what he meant, that a New Testament church must have New Testament music. The purpose of a church is to win people to Jesus Christ. A church music program is aimed at directing people to Jesus Christ.

I noted in the books on large churches that they had happy music, because the New Testament produces happy people. The Bible word is "blessed," which means happy. Blessed is the church that has a happy song, for they shall lead others to the Lord.

Music is the spiritual thermostat of a church, being both a regulator and reflector of the temperature. First, a thermostat incorporates a thermometer, which simply tells the heat level in a room. When I walk into a church that has nothing but classical anthems, I usually find no soul-winning activity. (There is nothing wrong with classical music, but it does not communicate to the heart of twentieth-century Americans; as a matter of fact, it turns them off, hence turning them away from God.)

Second, a thermostat regulates the furnace, hence the music can motivate people to soul winning and service. Use the ideas of his book to bring revival to your church. The author is extremely practical in such topics as how to select music, platform appearance, how to enlist musicians, and how to direct the program. Correctly applied, this book could be the instrument of revival for your church.

As important as music is, it is not the whole program of the church. Do not be deceived to think that correct music alone will bring revival to your church, for revival comes through agonizing prayer, Bible teaching, and serious Christian service. Harold Henniger, pastor, Canton Baptist Temple, best stated the balance: "You can't build a great church on music, but you can't build a great church *without* music."

The author is at once both profound and simple. His thoughts are so deep that you will have to read some paragraphs many times to understand the implications for your church. But, at the same time, you will find this a simple book, for music is simply opening the heart's door and expressing one's feeling in song. Music is the soul's expression.

I think Lindsay Terry is one of the best church musicians in America. I have been on the platform when he has led music programs, and I am amazed at his talents. I saw him lead members of the Atlanta Symphony Orchestra at the Regency Hyatt House for one of the most beautiful church banquets at which I have spoken. Lindsay Terry was dignified in his tuxedo and pulled expression from the musicians that moved our hearts. I have also heard him lead singing at a pastors' conference, motivating four thousand pastors. I am glad this artist has attempted to put his soul on paper, and I hope that you capture his expertise by reading this book.

Evangelistic music inspires me, even though I have a "tin ear." My children say I even talk flat. I once tried to sing in a quartet; and one summer I led singing in an evangelistic tent. I wanted to be a musician, but finally realized I did not have musical talent. God has given to Lindsay Terry the talent of music. His music speaks to my heart. I should go a step further and say that his music thrills me, for he can do what I can't. Even though I can't sing, I love to sing. And even though I can't play an instrument, I wish I could. I like the response this man pulls from me through his music.

May God set your heart to singing and, as you read the pages of this book, inspire you to "make a joyful noise unto the Lord."

Elmer L. Towns

1979

Franklin Road Baptist Church

AND CHRISTIAN SCHOOLS

Route 7 • Box 339 • Murfreesboro, Tennessee 37130 • Phone 890-0820

NEW AUDITORIUM

Bob Kelley
PASTOR

July 16, 1979

Dr. John R. Rice
Sword of the Lord
P.O. Box 1099
Murfreesboro, TN 37130

Dear Dr. Rice:

The best word I can find to describe Lindsay Terry's new book, "Church Music", is the word-----outstanding! Without a doubt it will be regarded as the best in its field. Dr. Terry has compiled a veritable college education in church music in one volume. He has run the gamut on church singing; from the man in the pew who can't sing a "lick" to the best evangelistic church choir in America. I say the book belongs in the hands of every music man in the land.

Sad to say, a great deal of our music in fundamental circles today presents a very sloppy image of our cause and beliefs or, on the other hand, it reeks with rock rhythmns. Terry's approach to church music is sane and scriptural. It aims at the heart of both saint and sinner. His book will make a musical program to be performed decently and in order and still maintain the life and vigor our churches so desperately need. I was deeply impressed with the overall goal of Brother Terry. His entire thrust and motivation in church music is to stir the heart for Jesus Christ. I am convinced that any church who uses this guide as a textbook will have a musical program with "drawing power".

Several subjects treated by Brother Terry are "lonely fields" in fundamentalism today. Very few fundamental churches have graded choirs for children, training in fundamentals of music for all ages and pastors who are not only involved in church music, but superintend the program.

One more thing, I feel should be said to manifest the thoroughness of this book is simply this---Terry exhalts the importance of spiritual music in the home. Singing homes are happy homes and great singers at home are great singers at church.

I trust my thoughts are helpful in your appraisal of this good book. I intend to buy one of the first copies sold at the Sword.

Sincerely in Christarist,

THE CHURCH WITH A ♥ FOR MURFREESBORO

Dr. Bob Kelley

Chapter I

What Does the Bible Say About Your Singing?

Music Is the Universal Language of Mankind and God Is the Author of This Language

The Bible first mentions music early in the writings God gave through Moses: Genesis 4:21, "Jubal. . .was the father of all such as handle the harp and organ." God intended that music should bless, encourage, calm and instruct man. He is to teach and admonish his fellowman with song. "Let the word of Christ dwell in you richly in all wisdom; teaching and admonishing one another in psalms and hymns and spiritual songs, singing with grace in your hearts to the Lord" (Col. 3:16).

Man Is to Praise God in Song

God declared to Job (38:7) that there was a time "when the morning stars sang together, and all the sons of God shouted for joy." Each one who comes to know God through His Son finds a song in his heart; God causes the sons of men on earth to sing together in praise to Him.

The Songs of Moses and the Children of Israel

Moses and the children of Israel sang together after God delivered them from bondage; their song is recorded in Exodus 15:1-19. Their joyful, victorious hearts were moved to singing. The same is true today.

A very unusual event is recorded in II Chronicles 5:12-14. A great throng was gathered for the dedication of the Temple by the children of Israel. The choir consisted of many thousands of Levites along with the instrumentalists, which included 120 priests playing trumpets. You will notice in these Scriptures that the Bible indicates that they were all in one place, at the east end of the altar. They were all arrayed in white garments. It must have been an awesome sight.

The Bible says, "When they lifted their voice with the trumpets and cymbals and instruments of musick," that they made one sound in praising God; in other words, they had so practiced and rehearsed their musical number that they were all able to sing together, even though they were numbered in the thousands. They lifted all of their voices as one great voice, with the musical instruments, and praised God in song. The Bible says that God was so pleased with their music that a great cloud filled the house of the Lord and the cloud was the glory of the Lord. The place was so overwhelmed with this demonstration of God's approval, that the priests could not stand to minister to the people. God's power came down after the "choir special."

How wonderful it would be if, in our churches when the choir stands to sing, each of their hearts were so in tune with each other and with the Lord that after the choir special the power of God would so overtake the place that His Spirit would be felt by every person in the congregation. God help it to be true in your church and in your life as a volunteer choir member.

The Psalms of David

The Book of Psalms is the hymnbook of the Bible. Written, for the most part, by David, the psalms seem to be songs given to men in times of trouble, oppression and deliverance.

Music in the New Testament

Music plays a wonderful role in the New Testament. Perhaps the first song came early at the birth of Christ. The angels may have "sung" together the message of His wondrous birth, although the Bible does not say this.

(a) *Singing of Jesus.* Jesus sang as a Child, at the usual gatherings for children or perhaps at school. He sang with His disciples—perhaps only once, but at least once. Matthew 26:30 says, "And when they had sung an hymn, they went out into the mount of Olives." He had been with His disciples during the Last Supper. He had blessed and broken the bread, had passed the bread and wine to them and they had eaten and drunk. After this sad occasion they sang a song of praise to God.

Jesus was soon to suffer as no man has suffered. He was nearing the time when He would become guilty before God, for every sin ever committed by any vile person on earth. He, alone, realized the extent of the excruciating, soul-rending pain that was about to be inflicted on His body, and then, laid onto that, the torment of His mind and soul. In the face of this horrible prospect, He wanted to sing. . .and what did He sing? A song of praise to God.

Only the power of God can cause a heart to sing in the face of great human suffering.

(b) *Every Christian should realize that he must do his own singing.* This truth is very forcibly driven home in Ephesians 5:18-20:

"And be not drunk with wine, wherein is excess; but be filled with the Spirit; Speaking to yourselves in psalms and hymns and spiritual songs, singing and making melody in your heart to the Lord; Giving thanks always for all things unto God and the Father in the name of our Lord Jesus Christ."

The same sentence that exhorts us to refrain from becoming drunk with wine, also commands us to be filled with the Holy Spirit of God. The same sentence also says that we are to speak to ourselves with psalms and hymns and spiritual songs and that we are to sing and make melody in our hearts to the Lord.

How could we obey a part of that Scripture and leave out the other? How could we refrain from becoming drunk with wine and be filled with the Spirit and then decide in our own hearts that we do not want to sing or praise His name? Just as no one could do my praying for me, no one could do my singing for me. No one could be filled with the Spirit of God for me and no one could do my singing for me. We must each do our own singing. It may not sound as pretty as we would like, but we must make some effort, at least in our hearts.

In more than five hundred places the Bible speaks of singers, musicians, musical instruments or makes some reference to our singing. It must be important to God. And if it is important to Him, then it must be important to you as a volunteer choir member.

Chapter II

Basic Ideals for a Good Choir

Aside from a salvation experience and a desire to serve Christ, a good volunteer choir member must become completely conversant with certain ideas and ideals concerning the music program of the church. The following outline, hopefully, will not oversimplify these ideals, but will set them down in such a way that even the most inexperienced can grasp these lessons.

The "Person" of the Music Program

The Bible tells us in Colossians 3:16, "Let the word of Christ dwell in you richly in all wisdom; teaching and admonishing one another in psalms and hymns and spiritual songs, singing with grace in your hearts to the Lord." Of course, the Word of Christ is the Bible. When we make the Bible the center of our lives, then Christ becomes the central figure of our being. He, in this way, becomes the "Person" of our music program. He must be the theme of our song. He and His message must be the cause of our singing. The end result of our songs must center around Him. Never should we sing anything in our church services, when trying to accomplish something spiritual, that's not based on the Scriptures.

When choir members are in tune with Christ they are in tune with each other, because He is not the author of confusion or division.

The Philosophy of the Music Program

There are times in your life when your total attention should be given to the music program of your church. Such times are the rehearsal periods and the performances in the church services. If you have chosen to be a choir member then you must give yourself to it, faithfully, as faithfully as your pastor gives himself to the work of your church. Of course, there are other times when other matters require your attention, but during those times mentioned above, you must be totally dedicated to the task of helping build a good music program.

As a choir member and a spiritual leader, consider the following bits of wisdom as suggested by Mr. Derric Johnson, a famous choir director.

(1) *Develop a sense of responsibility toward the people and their needs.* Romans 15:1 says, "We then that are strong ought to bear the infirmities of the weak, and not to please ourselves." When you decide to step onto the platform where the Word of God is preached, you assume a position of leadership, an awesome responsibility. The people in the pews have tremendous needs. You must sing with a heart full of love for them. Every person in your congregation has a need of some kind. Many of these needs can be helped or alleviated with your music and with the messages of your songs. You can ill-afford, before God, to do less than your best in fulfilling your responsibility.

(2) *Discover the difference between support and obligation.* Philippians 2:13 says, "For it is God which worketh in you both to will and to do of his good pleasure." How many choir members attend a weekly rehearsal out of obligation. . . "I'm obligated to do it, so I'll just do it." How pitiful when we sink to such a state of mind.

Your music should always be supportive of the church and the work of God under the direction and leadership of the pastor. Your support of the minister of music should be forthright and positive. Only when we collectively and actively support the work of our church, in whatever area we are engaged, can we be rewarded and blessed as individuals.

(3) *Dedicate yourself to positive leadership attitudes.* . . .John 1:42: "Thou art. . .thou shalt be."

Because you appear on the church platform each week, you assume a position of Christian leadership. You may say, "I don't want to be a Christian leader, just because I want to be in the choir." You have the privilege of saying that, but it doesn't alter the situation. You're still a leader. You must think as a leader, and yet, your "followship" must be unquestioned. Only good followers can become good leaders.

Each of us one day will give an account of our leadership. You may say, "I don't want anybody looking at my life. I want to live my own life and let others live as they want." Again, let me say that you have the privilege of saying that, but it does not alter the fact that others are watching your life. And you will give an account of your leadership.

A young man once wrote a poem that goes:

> It is only just a minute,
> But there's sixty seconds in it.
> Didn't choose it, can't refuse it;
> I'll give an account if I abuse it.
> It is only just a minute
> But there's sixty seconds in it.

Just as you and I will give an account of our time here on this earth, each of us will give an account of our leadership.

(4) *Verbalize your dreams.* It will help you as a choir member to actually tell God what you want your life to be like. If you want to be a faithful choir member, then tell Him so. If you want to be supportive of His work, which includes the work of the church, the pastor, and the music director, then tell Him so—out loud. It will do you good to hear it come from your own lips. If we ask in faith then God will give us the desires of our heart.

Let me illustrate. The Apostle Peter was one day out on the sea with other followers of Jesus. The winds were high, the waves were dashing, and all in the boat must have been fearful.

Presently, they saw One coming toward them walking on the water. They perceived that it was Jesus.

At that point, Peter verbalized his dreams. First of all, he must have thought to himself, "Wow! I would surely like to do that; it has always been impossible, but now I see Christ walking on the water so I think I'll ask Him to let me do it, also." And then Peter said, "Lord, if it be thou, bid me come unto thee on the water." Apparently Jesus' attitude was, "O.K., Peter, if that is what you want, and you have asked it, then I'll let you do that." Peter then got out of the boat and began to walk. He was not successful all the way to Jesus, but when he became fearful and began to sink, Jesus helped him. . .and He will help you.

If you want to become a good choir member, just say, "Lord, help me to be the best choir member that I can possibly be. Help me to be victorious as a Christian leader in the choir of our church."

(5) *Challenge yourself to excel in performance and lifestyle.* The Bible says in I Timothy 4:12: "Be thou an example of the believers, in word, in conversation, in charity, in spirit, in faith, in purity." It is quite easy for us to live victorious lives while at church, but in our communities and behind closed doors of our own homes the load becomes heavier and our faithfulness is tested. You cannot be victorious on the platform of your church and live a defeated Christian life in your community or in your home.

Study the ideas above and make them a part of your total attitude.

The Place of the Music Program

The preaching of the Word of God is always given first place in any church and rightly so. All of our activities in the church center around the Word of God. Music should take second place.

When you consider the tremendous amounts of God's money spent on the music program for such items as pianos, organs, hymnals, choir music, salaries, etc., then it should be placed second to the preaching. When you consider the thousands of collective hours spent each year by choir members, who faithfully engage in practice sessions, then it should be recognized as a very worthwhile part of the total church program. When you consider the multiplied thousands of collective hours spent by the congregation, singing hymns and listening to the music of the church, then you realize more time and effort is spent in the music ministry than in any other church activity other than the preaching.

The Preparation With the Music

During each service the minds of the people must be prepared for the preaching of the Word of God. Since we sing scriptural messages, then we are preparing them for the preaching of the Bible with messages taken from the Bible. This is in keeping with Colossians 3:16.

There are three groups of people who need to be prepared for the sermon.

(1) *The congregation.* When five hundred people are gathered for a church service then five hundred minds are going in as many different directions. We must pull these minds into the service. It can be done with music. We begin to prepare hearts as the choir marches in. If the tread of each choir member is definite and firm and somewhat hurried the audience settles back with an attitude that "something is about to take place." And then from the opening choir number to the solo, just before the message, minds are brought into the service and prepared for the sermon.

A teenage boy may be thinking of a lost football game. A junior boy may be thinking of a swap that he's going to make after the service. A businessman, perhaps, is consumed with the idea of a "big deal" next week. An elderly lady is very near the gates of Heaven and a woman expecting a little baby is the most miserable lady in the church. They must be brought into the service. Do it with the music.

When a music director, with the help of the choir, can bring the minds of the people to a point ready for a message from the Word of God, then his task has been well done during that particular service.

(2) *The choir.* Each choir member should be made ready for the sermon by the pastor. He can only be ready if he can honestly and earnestly pray, "Dear Lord, I have done my best. I have been faithful to the choir rehearsals. Now, use our songs to be a blessing to others."

(3) *The pastor should be prepared.* Pastors often are embarrassed because of lack of preparation and a lack of real dedication to the music ministry on the part of those who have chosen to be involved in it.

Pastors may invite visitors to attend services, only to have themselves embarrassed with an ill-prepared music ministry. Many times pastors have said, "What in the world am I going to do? I invite visitors and the choir has a 'hallelujah breakdown.' It becomes evident that they haven't practiced sufficiently. A duet or a quartet perform so poorly, far below their capability, that by the time I am ready to preach my stomach is tied in knots."

We must be willing to spend the necessary time to make our music program acceptable to God Himself.

Each musical number may not "knock you off your chair," but, if the pastor realizes that his people have done their best in preparation then his heart is blessed because of their efforts.

The Purpose of the Music Program

Every aspect of our lives should have a purpose and an intent. The purpose of the volunteer choir is:

(1) To sing for souls. As you perform you must love the souls of men sitting before you. There's an old quote, "Sing your song prayerfully, it may be used to save a soul."

(2) To draw people to the church. Good music draws good musicians.

(3) To obey the Scriptures. The Bible commands that we are to sing. We are simply doing what God has asked us to do.

(4) To use a great number of people in the program of the church. Children and teenagers may not be able to teach Sunday school classes, be bus captains, visit in the hospitals, or a variety of other things, but they can give their testimonies in song. When

it is done in an exciting and an unusual manner, it is of great service to the cause of Christ.

The Planning of the Music Program

God says that we are to do all things "decently and in order." This must include our music ministry. Our best laid plans, sometimes, have a way of going astray, but the person who has the best plan usually will have the best music. Especially is this true if great effort is put forth to carry out the plan.

A choir director must plan his rehearsals and his music services which often include a variety of musical offerings.

An organist must plan offertories, introductions of choir specials, preludes, postludes, etc.

Individuals involved in the performances must enter into the planning.

If we are to offer God, in our services, that which is "without spot or blemish," then we must work at our plan.

The Payoff of a Good Music Program

There is a great payoff in a good music program, including:

(1) The love and appreciation of the church for a job well done.

(2) Souls are won to Christ.

(3) Christian hearts are blessed.

(4) The Saviour will say, "Well done, thou good and faithful servant."

The above basic ideas and ideals are intended for a choral group of any size.

Chapter III

What Is Evangelistic Music?

Pastors across America cry for a musical program that is vibrant and alive, a heart-warming program that *lives* as it projects a message of life. Never has there been such need for music that moves upon the hearts of people as there is today; never such need for. . .

music that the common man can grasp and understand;
music that knows no boundary;
music that speaks to the masses;
music enjoyed by the uneducated as well as the educated,
the rich and the poor,
the high and the low,
the children and the adults,
the teens and the grandparents. . .

The sacred classics are beautiful and they should have a time and place in our lives, but an evangelistic church service is not the time or the place. Consider these three reasons:

(1) *The classics tend to call attention to the performance.*

All too often the real message of the composition becomes lost in great swelling chords and oft-repeated phrases. The actual makeup of the composition becomes dominant. This glorifies the song and not the Saviour. Every Christian musical presentation should leave the audience more aware of the message of the song than of the excellence of the performance—not that both should not be favorably accepted.

(2) *The classics lend themselves to formal service.*

Formalism and evangelism do not go hand in hand. Formalism soothes and deadens; evangelism arouses and awakens. A pastor

cannot expect to arouse to positive action a congregation lulled
into complacency by the musical portion of the service.
Congregations, generally speaking, are not deeply moved by the
sacred classics.

(3) *The classics are too difficult for the ordinary church choir.*

Since most choirs, especially in smaller churches, are made up
of relatively untrained singers, few of them are able to master the
classics. A choir should not perform in a service any music that
cannot be learned well. Nothing distresses the pastor and the
congregation more than to hear the pitiful struggles of an ill-
prepared choir. With time at a premium and rehearsal time
limited, it is far better to use music that singers can learn rapidly
and perform well. They will then take personal pride in the choir
and their part in the service. This is a *must* for an evangelistic at-
mosphere.

The classics should certainly be used and appreciated, but in a
special program or concert in which they can be presented for
audience appreciation of both composition and performance.

The music program of any church should be given as thorough
care as humanly possible. Evangelistic music can be done in a
way that will challenge the best musicians, and still be understood and enjoyed by the entire audience.

To further define evangelistic music, consider the following
characteristics:

It Tells a Story

Many songs relate a story or are in story form. These are effective because they are usually filled with human interest.
Everyone loves a story, and stories set to music are retained in
the mind more readily. Some story-songs are: "Then Jesus
Came," "The Stranger of Galilee," "At Calvary," "The Old Rug-
ged Cross" and "Christ Arose." The most effective of these are
based on the Scriptures, as opposed to others with only "religious
flavor."

It Gives a Testimony

Truly some of the most blessed songs are those that bear

testimony of faith in the Saviour. Songs of testimony have been used to bring many people to a knowledge of Christ. These songs, like all others in the services, must have a definite quality of sincerity. Some of these are: "Saved, Saved," "Standing on the Promises," "Amazing Grace," and "The Solid Rock." The titles indicate that the songs are favorites of people across America and have been used of God to touch the hearts of countless numbers of people.

It Is a Prayer

Many best-loved songs and hymns are prayers set to music. A whole congregation can pray together by singing a prayer. A prayer song is always addressed to the Heavenly Father, to Christ or to the Holy Spirit. The music director or the pastor should occasionally remind the congregation to think of the words they are singing. It must hurt the heart of God for His people to be praying to Him in the words of a song and yet hardly knowing what they are asking of Him or what they are saying to Him.

Polls across America show that high on the list of favorite songs are some of the prayers set to music. One is "Rock of Ages." Some other songs that would be considered prayers are: "Saviour Like a Shepherd Lead Us," "I Am Thine, O Lord," "I Need Thee Every Hour," and "My Faith Looks Up to Thee."

It Teaches

One of the grandest uses of sacred music is in teaching people the Word of God. From pre-school years in the Sunday school and on through life, people are taught the truths of God through sacred songs. One reason that songs are such good teachers is that people hear them over and over again. Repetition is like mucilage; it seals and causes a message to stick in the minds of those who take part in the singing. Many a wayward person has come to the Lord Jesus Christ later in life because he remembered a song his godly mother had sung many years before. He had been taught about God with a song.

People cannot be taught through sacred music unless it carries a definite message or lesson. The following songs have wonderful messages needed by every person: "There Is a Fountain Filled With Blood," and "Calvary Covers It All."

Sunday school would not be nearly so effective if it were not for the "little" songs that the children are taught. They learn Bible truths with songs.

It Praises

There is a distinction between hymns and gospel songs. A hymn is a song of praise to Jesus, the Heavenly Father, or the Holy Spirit. Although many people lump all sacred songs into one category—hymns—this is not technically correct. The gospel songs tell a story or give a message of some kind, and a hymn is directed to God.

Much is said in the Bible about praising God with the voice as well as with instruments. In Colossians 3:16 the Bible seems to make a distinction between songs and hymns.

Many hymns of praise are evangelistic in scope. For example: "All Hail the Power of Jesus Name," "Glory to His Name," and "Praise Him, Praise Him" are all wonderful songs of praise.

It Expresses Love

God looks on the heart, and an expression of love in any form is acceptable to Him. In my opinion the most beautiful way to express love to the Saviour is through songs—usually prayer songs, although every prayer song is not necessarily a song of love. Consider the following: "O Love That Wilt Not Let Me Go," "Love Lifted Me," and "Jesus Loves Even Me."

Surely, a most beautiful sight to the Saviour is a group of His people, gathered together with bowed heads and sincere hearts, singing. . .

> My Jesus, I love Thee, I know Thou art mine.
> For Thee all the follies of sin I resign.
> My gracious Redeemer, my Saviour art Thou;
> If ever I loved Thee, my Jesus, 'tis now.

It Warns

Songs that warn of judgment to come are not beautiful songs, nor are they enjoyable to sing, but they need to be used occasionally. They do not bless the hearts of Christians as other songs, but they still need to be sung. Words of warning to those without Christ or to those living afar from God stay in the mind longer, perhaps, because they are usually set to a haunting melody. In many cases, the combination of the words and the melody causes the song to reach great heights.

Songs of warning are not as numerous as others, but consider a few: "The Great Judgment Morning," "Have You Counted the Cost?" and "There's a Great Day Coming"—to name a few.

It Anticipates

Songs of anticipation are songs about Heaven, Christ's return, or His eternal reign. Every Christian should continually anticipate the coming of Christ, when we shall be with Him. Songs about Heaven should not be reserved for funerals, but should be used often in services and in daily lives. Following are some examples: "Zion's Hill," "One Day," "We Shall See His Lovely Face," and "At the End of the Road."

It Assures

Sacred music would not be complete without songs of assurance that help Christians to know their salvation is steadfast, and to be sure that God sees, knows, and cares for them. Singing in time of trial or darkness brightens any situation, reminding people that God is still on the throne. It is grand and glorious to sing in the midst of trouble, even as Paul and Silas sang, with bleeding backs and feet fast in the stocks.

"Hallelujah for the Cross," "Blessed Assurance," "A Shelter in the Time of Storm," "He Leadeth Me," and "I Must Tell Jesus" are a few songs that express assurance.

It Blesses

Singing, or hearing a song beatifully sung, has brought great thrills or blessings. No thrill or blessing has exceeded that of hearing "The Loveliness of Christ" sung by a blind singer. Music in evangelistic church services is marvelous in its blessing to those who hear or who take part as congregation or special singers. While church music should chiefly be geared to help reach the lost, it should also be for the blessing and strength for the born again.

Of the thousands of songs in this category, here are a few: "Jesus Is All the World to Me," "How Firm a Foundation," "Jesus, the Very Thought of Thee," and "The Name of Jesus."

It Comforts

Many elderly people, especially, find comfort in wonderful sacred songs that tell of Heaven. Others, not so elderly, find comfort and strength in such songs as "Safe in the Arms of Jesus," "Lead Me Gently Home," and "No One Ever Cared for Me Like Jesus." A world filled with sorrow, heartache and trials would suffer a great loss if deprived of these or the thousands of other wonderful songs of comfort.

It Prepares

Life on earth is a continual preparation. The Christian's greatest task, besides winning others to Christ, is preparing to spend eternity with God. Not only should we prepare for Heaven, but we should be preparing to live better lives for Christ here on the earth.

Examples of songs that help to prepare are: "Break Thou the Bread of Life," "Faith Is the Victory," and "Beneath the Cross of Jesus."

It Gives an Invitation

The most important time in an evangelistic service is the invitation time. The songs have been sung, the Scriptures have been read, the announcements have been given, prayer has been made, and the sermon preached. Then comes the time of invitation—the time when men are invited to come and make a public profession of faith in the Lord. Songs that can be used at this time are: "Softly and Tenderly," "Jesus, I Come," "Just As I Am," and "Only Trust Him."

It Exhorts

One of the most famous of all hymn stories is that behind "Stand Up, Stand Up for Jesus," a song of exhortation. This song was born in a time of revival, when Dudley Tyng lay dying after a horrible accident. At that time his exhortation to the young men who worked with him was to *STAND UP FOR JESUS*. Another wonderful song of exhortation is "We're Marching to Zion."

It Expresses Gratitude

If God's people have any fault more continually with them than others, it is ungratefulness. This attitude could be changed through congregational use of such songs as "O Happy Day," "Count Your Blessings," and "Come Ye Thankful People, Come."

Songs of gratitude should be a part of our church services.

It Strengthens

In these days, and in the days that lie ahead, Christians can find help in singing songs that call their attention to the strength that God gives. Hundreds of songs, perhaps even thousands, do this, but consider these few: "Dare to Be a Daniel," "In Times Like These," "If I Gained the World," and "When I Kneel Down to Pray."

Evangelistic music does all of the things discussed here and more. Considered collectively or individually, evangelistic songs are what the people of America need. Since this is true, it behooves every church to make her music program evangelistic.

The following are some thoughts on evangelistic music by Dr. Jack Hyles, pastor of the famed First Baptist Church of Hammond, Indiana.

THE REAL NEED OF EVANGELISTIC MUSIC

Music is one of the most important forms of praise. The word "hallelujah," which means "praise the Lord," is pronounced the same in all languages. The last five Psalms begin and end with the words "Praise the

Lord." In Psalm 74:21, the poor and needy are admonished to praise the Lord. In Psalm 148:12, the young and the old are to praise the Lord. In the same verse, men and women are to praise the Lord. Paul and Silas praised Him at midnight as they sang. In II Chronicles 29:30, the Levites sang praises to God. Peter admonishes us in I Peter 2:9 to show forth His praises.

In no way can we praise the Lord better and more sweetly than with music. A song was sung after the Israelites had crossed the Red Sea. When Deborah and Barak had defeated the forces of Sisera, a song was sung. Mary sang when she learned of the coming of the Christ Child.

Once a man in my church who managed a cafeteria told me to visit his establishment at the noon hour. He instructed his organist to play a waltz. The people literally waltzed through and slowly picked up their food. Then he instructed her to play a march. The people very quickly and with jerky motions picked up their food. He said, "You see, Pastor, what influence music has on people." Because this is true, church music should influence people for the right. Dead music can tranquilize the audience before a sermon. For that matter, it can tranquilize the preacher, too. Rock music with religious words can turn a service toward the sensual. There is nothing more vital than proper music in the church, music that appeals to the heart, music that gives a message, music that is spiritual both in lyrics and in musical setting. May God use this publication to help stabilize our churches musically.

Chapter IV

Music, an Arm of Evangelism

Music that cannot be considered a part of the total evangelistic outreach of the church should not be used in the church. There are so many ways that music can be an arm of evangelism in our churches.

The Sunday Services of the Church

Music that incorporates a message of salvation can cause people in the pews to literally yield their hearts to Christ on the spot. Many people, presently not living dedicated lives, were at one time faithful in church attendance. Thus, when they hear the great hymns and gospel songs sung during a church service, their hearts are strangely warmed and moved toward spiritual rededication or actual conversion: the message that follows is the clincher.

The Children's Choirs

Children's hearts are young and pliable and easily moved, especially through music. A two-year-old has often learned more through the children's songs in the toddler's department of the Sunday school than from the spoken word, because these musical messages can be repeated at home, on the playground, or in the bedroom at night. Family trips are often more cheerful because of songs that the children sing, which they learned in the children's choir.

There are some ways to reach children during the children's choir rehearsal that have nothing to do with the musical aspect of their meeting.

Devotional Time

Because the Beginner, Primary, and Junior choirs need several breaks during rehearsal, a devotional period can be used effectively. During this devotional period several practical lessons can be taught, and the plan of salvation can be presented periodically. On several occasions the author has presented the plan of salvation in the children's choir. Those who were interested in learning how to be saved remained after the others had gone, when more time was available for counseling. But the first contact with them was made during the devotional time of the children's choir.

Visits in the Home

A dedicated children's choir director has a perfect entrance into the home of a choir member. Imagine the choir director walking up to the front door of a home, knocking, and when the mother answers the door, saying, "I am Mrs. Smith, director of the Primary Choir at First Baptist Church. Your son, Johnny, is in my choir, and he is such a fine boy I wanted to come and meet

his parents. Are you Mrs. Jones?" The director would not be
denied entrance into one out of ten thousand homes that she approached with an introduction of that nature. Even though the
parents may already be Christians, she can invite them to the
services, and they may become church members because their
little boy became a member of a children's choir at the church.

Music Draws New People

At one church where I was minister of music, in Miami,
Florida, whole families joined the church because of the teen
choir that sang every Sunday morning there. Adults want their
teens to be engaged in the activities of the church. Such participation assures parents that the young lives will be pointed in
the right direction. A large teen choir can attract not only
parents, but other teens as well.

Services in Other Locations

There are numerous opportunities for church musicians to be
of service to Christ outside the church services. They may be
asked, or may ask, to sing in rest homes or jails.

Many forgotten souls are housed in the numerous rest homes of
virtually every city in America. Their spirits can be lifted to
great heights with your music.

The prisons are an ever-increasing mission field. The inmates
have all had some appreciation for music in the outside world.
Share your musical testimony with them. In most cases, the
wardens will be delighted to arrange your visit.

Choir tours are very popular these days.

These opportunities for appearing at special civic affairs are
too numerous to mention. Some are (1) state legislature houses;
(2) civic club meetings; (3) shopping centers; (4) street or park
open-air services; or (5) home meetings—and the list could go on
and on.

Chapter V

A Concept of Church Music

By Dr. Lee Roberson, Pastor
Highland Park Baptist Church, Chattanooga, Tennessee

It is a delight for me to write on the subject of church music. I have been preaching for almost forty-five years, but have had an intense interest in music from the time of my conversion. I remember the first song that I led, in the old Cedar Creek Baptist Church in Louisville, Kentucky. I remember the battles I had between preaching and singing in the early part of my ministry. I had such delight in singing that I felt this was the ministry God had for me. But, no, God had a definite purpose for my life, and I rejoice that I accepted His way.

What a great calling is that of music! How marvelously God uses men and women in the proclamation of divine truth through music.

Every singer should get the best in training. Know music. Let the learning process continue throughout life. Good teachers are available in most cities. It costs money to take lessons, but it is worth it. Study the methods for producing the best of music from poor "sinners saved by grace."

The building of a great choir is dependent upon the leader and his ability. He must stir others, and he must challenge them to give their best. Good leadership solves the problem of attendance and also the problem of producing God-glorifying music.

There is so much to be said upon this subject that I prefer to outline briefly what I think music should do. I am referring to the greatest of all music—sacred music.

1. *Music should inspire.* Music should inspire us to noble living. The proper kind of music should cause us to hate lowly, sinful things and encourage us to strive for the noblest life.

Music should inspire us to a dedication of life. How many of us would have to testify that we have come to the place of dedication through the message of a well-selected and properly presented song?

Music should inspire us to service, unselfish service. Music, based upon the Word of God, should call forth our human best for His divine purposes.

2. *Music should encourage.* We all have times of discouragement. Despondency often besets us. David had some low, dark hours, but he had a song in his heart. Read the Psalms carefully; you will see the evidence of this. Fanny Crosby had lonely, discouraging hours. She never saw the light of day or the beauty of God's flowers or the loveliness of the sunset. Fanny Crosby received encouragement through her God, and her songs reveal this. Dr. Charles Weigle wrote his best songs in the times of his greatest gloom. "No One Ever Cared for Me Like Jesus" came out of a dark hour. "I Have Found a Hiding Place" came from a time of despondency.

As the songwriters found encouragement, even in difficult hours, to write songs, so we should find encouragement in music to lift us to higher planes in hours of dejection and despair.

I remember, when I first began my work as a preacher, the blessedness of the song, "Just When I Need Him Most." Down through the years this song has ever given me encouragement.

3. *Music should teach.* Yes, music should teach us the love of God, salvation by grace, eternal security, justification by faith, the second coming of Christ, Heaven, and Hell; and the great doctrines of the Word should be made plain through our songs.

There is something wrong with a song that teaches nothing. (We had better check some of the modern-day sacred songs. Many of them teach nothing at all.) Bible teaching must be interwoven in all sacred gospel songs and hymns.

4. *Music should ever point to the Saviour.* Yes, "faith cometh by hearing, and hearing by the word of God." But as songs are based upon the Word of God, they will have the message to aid people to see Christ.

Many of the simple songs that we sing so often express the thought I have in mind. I refer to songs like "My Faith Looks Up to Thee," "Amazing Grace, How Sweet the Sound," "My Hope Is Built on Nothing Less Than Jesus' Blood and Righteousness," and "What Can Wash Away My Sin? Nothing but the Blood of Jesus." The Word of God can be preached through songs, as well as through the spoken Word. We must use in our churches songs that will continually place before sinners Christ, the only Saviour. The beauty of melody must sometimes be sacrificed for a song with a definite, pointed emphasis on Christ Jesus.

Yes, music should inspire; music should encourage; music should teach; and music should point to Christ the Saviour! I am sure there is much more that can be said upon this subject, but I am merely touching what I feel is primary. Every church should seek to present the finest and the best in music Sunday after Sunday. This requires time, money, energy, and dedication. It requires death to self, the filling of the Spirit, and a constant looking-up for divine approval.

Now, permit me to close these comments with two verses from the Word of God:

"Speaking to yourselves in psalms and hymns and spiritual songs, singing and making melody in your hearts to the Lord; Giving thanks always for all things unto God and the Father in the name of our Lord Jesus Christ."—Eph. 5:19,20.

Chapter VI

Essentials for Being a Good Choir Member

Presented in this chapter are eight prime requisites for choir members that should receive special attention.

Faithfulness. The Bible has a great deal to say about the faithfulness of Christians. The rewards are great for those who just stick to the job: those who are right in their places when they are supposed to be. Of all the essentials that will be discussed, this one is first and foremost.

Punctuality: Be on time, always!

Approach the platform carefully. As the door opens for the entrance of the choir, the attitude of each should be one of prayerfulness, anticipation, excitement, and appreciation. Many visitors decide that they are going to enjoy the service by the way the choir marches in. The entrance of the choir should be carefully rehearsed.

Once a choir member is in his place his attention should be given wholly to those things happening on the platform.

Be alert. Always be ready to perform. When it is time for the congregational singing, have your hymnal ready. Anticipate the singing of the choir special and be on your toes. Be flexible in case some change in the practiced procedure is needed.

Watch your posture. It costs something to be a good choir member. One of those "costs" is some personal comfort. As a member of the choir you must sit up very straight with both feet on the floor, never calling attention to any casualness on your part. While singing, always keep the shoulders high and the head erect.

Be attentive. Thumbing through hymnals, the Bible, unless when asked, writing notes or generally being inattentive are distracting to those sitting in the congregation. A good choir member will at all times be interested in every aspect of the service including the announcements, no matter how lengthy.

Especially during the invitation should the choir members watch the choir director and give one hundred per cent attention to prayerful singing.

Watch the director. During the performance *watch* the *director.* Books should be held in such a position as to allow the singer to very quickly glance up at the director or to see him out of the peripheral vision.

Most congregations are aware that choir members are to watch the director, so if this is violated, it reflects on both the director and the choir member.

Sing with a love for souls. People respond to love when they are moved by no other stimulus. If you as a choir member love the souls of men and sing with them in mind then it will somehow show in your face.

Chapter VII

The Adult Choir

The adult or senior choir is the best and most widely used in most churches; therefore, consideration should be given to this choir first. Nine points of consideration are listed.

Rebuilding an Existing Choir

Most churches, however large or small, have some kind of an adult choir that is used in at least one service on Sunday. Perhaps, for some reason, this choir should be rebuilt. The music survey may provide prospects for rebuilding an existing choir.

First of all, the existing choir should be surveyed to determine
its strong and weak points. Begin reorganizing as though a brand
new choir were being formed. Recruit as many new members as
possible, as soon as possible. Set down choir rules and regulations and let the choir know these will be kept. In general, the
choir should understand that they are passing into a new era,
and things will be done differently henceforth. This action must
be taken in Christian love, with much diplomacy.

Many of the following suggestions about building a new choir
may also be used in rebuilding an existing choir.

Starting a New Choir

Set a meeting time when as many prospective choir members
as possible can come. Contact prospects whose name and phone
numbers are on the survey blanks. A good accompanist and acceptable rehearsal time should have already been chosen.

The first meeting gives opportunity for the director to set down
the rules and regulations and map out future plans for the choir.
The director should convey his own real enthusiasm about this
ministry.

The Weekly Rehearsal

1. *Start and stop on time.* The choir will appreciate this consideration and attention to punctuality. People in the jet age are
busy. If they know they will be able to start practicing at a given
time and stop at a set time, they will not hesitate to set aside this
time for practice. Keep their confidence by keeping your starting
and stopping time rigid.

2. *Use several selections at each rehearsal.* Start rehearsals or
practice times (whichever you prefer to call them) by singing
through each hymn for the following Sunday's congregational
singing. Spend the next fifteen to twenty minutes on the choir arrangement for the next Sunday's services. Then go from song to
song, using four to six songs in each rehearsal, spending about
ten minutes on each.

There are two reasons for using several selections. First, it breaks the monotony; perhaps more important, it allows them to practice a song at four or five rehearsals. This is much more important than spending an hour and a half or two hours on one or two arrangements. If a choir member has to miss rehearsal, he has already practiced the song in three or four other rehearsals; therefore he should be able to perform consistently with the choir. Close rehearsal by repeating next Sunday's arrangement.

3. *Have a few breaks in the practice time.* Do not sing a choir hard for extended periods, particularly when working with untrained voices. They need a rest, or "breather," occasionally.

4. *Prepare the accompanists ahead of time.* Don't embarrass the accompanists by putting new music in front of them and expecting them to play it the first time they see it. They will appreciate a chance to go over it in privacy a few times before coming to the choir rehearsal.

5. *Don't be too serious all through the rehearsal.* Be light and jovial. That is not to say that the director should try to be a clown, but he should try to be lighthearted once in awhile, letting the singers relax.

6. *Demand discipline.* Without being a tyrant, command and demand strict choir discipline. You cannot get the allotted work done in rehearsal without good discipline.

7. *Choose a good place to practice.* Many choirs, by necessity, have to practice in the choir loft in which they will be performing. This can be a drawback, because of the largeness of the room. If possible, go to another room which gives good sound for hearing all parts and voices.

8. *The choir director should keep ahead of his choir.* Keep ahead musically, by knowing the arrangements in advance of rehearsal. Keep ahead by having plenty of music for them to work on at each rehearsal. A well-planned rehearsal assures confidence on the part of the director. If his morale is high, he can convey to the choir a high spirit of enthusiasm.

Sources of Material

Several companies can supply good evangelistic choir arrangements. Their musicians take a simple hymn or gospel song and change it into a beautiful, challenging choir song. Following is a list of several such companies and their addresses.

1. Singspiration, Inc.
   Zondervan Publishing House
   Grand Rapids, Michigan 49506
2. John T. Benson Publishing Company
   1625 Broadway Street
   Nashville, Tennessee 37203
3. Manna Music Inc.
   1328 N. Highland Ave.
   Hollywood, California 90028
4. Mosie Lister Publications
   Tampa, Florida
5. The Rodeheaver, Hall-Mack Company
   Winona Lake, Indiana 46590
6. Gospel Publishing House
   Springfield, Missouri
7. Lillenas Publishing Company
   Kansas City, Missouri
8. Broadman Press
   Nashville, Tennessee 37203
9. Accent, Inc.
   Box 37, Station C
   Grand Rapids, Michigan 49506

Keeping Contact With the Members

Any good choir director will keep up with his choir members. Have the choir secretary check the roll at each rehearsal. If a choir member is not present, find out why. Ask the choir members to call if they cannot be present for a rehearsal. Periodic choir letters to all participants encourages faithfulness. Absentee letters will keep nonattendance at a minimum.

Recruiting New Members

As new members join the church, find out if they would like to sing in the choir. Keep working on the prospects received from the survey; contact and enlist them, if possible. A choir grows in the same way as a Sunday school class—by personal contact.

Motivating Faithfulness

Regularly stress faithfulness. Remind the members that every choir is made up of individuals; if individuals are not present, the choir is not present. Help them realize that it is just as important for them to be in place as for the choir director to be in his place. God rewards faithfulness. Place the choir on a very high plane. Guide them to see that this is their place of service, and that it is a very important place of service.

Music Training

A few moments during each of several choir rehearsals may be used to teach some of these facts and skills, or you may call attention to certain music fundamentals at rehearsals each week. Either way, strive to help all members attain knowledge of the fundamentals of music; they will be better choir members.

Chapter VIII

The Teenage Choir

Special attention has been drawn to my music ministry, in which I have been able, with God's help, to build three large teenage choirs. Some people find this almost unbelievable today. I contend that teenagers are the same in this day as in every other. Of course, they have different motivations, different environments, but basically they are the same.

In building teenage choirs we use essentially the same system as with an adult choir; yet it is quite different in some ways, because teens are involved.

Starting a New Choir

It is best not to rebuild an existing choir, but to dissolve it and start anew.

1. *Set a meeting time.* Set the time at three or four weeks ahead. Go to every teenage department of the Sunday school telling them of your plans to build a large teenage choir, letting them know the date of the first meeting. Make sure they know that this is not a practice time; it is a meeting with those interested in filling out applications to become members of a teenage choir.

Announce that every person desiring membership in the new choir must fill out an application blank; the applications will be processed and all applicants will be notified as to whether or not they are accepted as members in the new choir. Talk it up big; make them realize that this is one of the most important teenage functions in the church, because it is.

When the day arrives for this first meeting do not be alarmed if you do not have a large crowd present; you will have, by the time several months have gone by. Just make sure, prior to the meeting, to build it up and boost it in every way possible.

2. *Give out the applications at the first meeting,* asking teens to take them home and prayerfully fill them out. The application is divided into three parts. The first part has primarily the same information on it as the church music survey. The second, and perhaps the most important part, is this: "State briefly your reasons for wanting to be a member of the Teen Choraliers." The reason must be a Christian one. The director must determine if the teenagers' motives are right, if they really want to be in the choir for spiritual reasons or just because the gang is there. Of course, some will be motivated for that reason, but at least they know they are supposed to be there for spiritual reasons. If an application comes back without a spiritual reason stated, it should be rejected and returned to the teenager with the tactful ex-

planation that his reason must be Christian, since choir is a service for Christ.

3. *Consider the seven rules* in the last part of the application. The rules are these:

a. I will strive to be on time for every rehearsal.

b. I will strive to keep my mind on the business at hand during rehearsal as well as during the services.

c. I'll help to preserve the present conditions of all materials used, books, hymnals, and sheet music.

d. I will refrain from unnecessary talking during all rehearsals.

e. I will recognize the authority of the conductor in all matters pertaining to the choir.

f. Realizing that unnecessary activity in the choir during the church services distracts the attention of the audience, I will refrain from writing notes, chewing gum, thumbing through hymnals and being generally inattentive.

g. I will strive to be present for every rehearsal and performance.

The application is closed with this: "Having carefully read the above regulations, I prayerfully affix my signature." There is a place for the signature and the phone number. The phone number is of vital importance as the chief medium of contact.

4. *Receive the completed applications* at a meeting held about a week after they were taken home and filled out. At this time, map out plans for the choir. Let them know what is expected of them, and just exactly what they can expect from the director. Tell them exactly in what services they will sing. Share recreational or outing plans. Tell about the contests being planned.

5. *Choose a good name for the choir,* one that teenagers can be proud of.

The teen choir should be the service choir for one service during the week, if possible—perhaps on Sunday evening or Wednesday evening.

6. *Place the choir on a high plane.* Make sure the teens know the seriousness of building a good choir, and that they are ex-

pected to work hard to make the choir something of which they can be proud, something that will bring honor to Christ and to the church.

Here is the application blank for membership that I use.

TEEN CHOIR
APPLICATION BLANK

NAME _____ AGE_____ BIRTH DATE MO. ____ DAY ____ YR.

ADDRESS _____ CITY_____ SCHOOL _____

Are you a Christian?_____ Are you a church member?_____Where? _____
Are you a member of the Sunday School?_____What Dept.? _____
Teacher?_____
Do you have a low_____ or high_____voice?
Have you had voice training?_____
Do you play an instrument?_____Name the instrument._____
Have you been a member of a choir before? _____Where?_____
Name the choir(s) in which you participated. _____

State briefly your reasons for wanting to be a member of the "TEEN CHOIR."

_____

The Bible teaches that all things done for Christ should be done decently and in order; therefore, the following rules and regulations have been instituted:

As a member of the "TEEN CHOIR," I will:

1. Strive to be on time for every rehearsal.
2. Strive to keep my mind on the business at hand during rehearsals as well as during the services.
3. Help to preserve the present conditon of all materials used—books, hymnals, sheet music, etc.
4. Refrain from unnecessary talking during all rehearsals.
5. Recognize the authority of the conductor in all matters pertaining to choir.
6. Realize that unnecessary activities during the church services distract the attention of those in the audience; therefore, I will refrain from writing "notes," chewing gum, thumbing through hymnals, and generally being inattentive.
7. Strive to be present for every rehearsal and performance.

Having carefully read the above regulations, I prayerfully affix my signature.

_____

Phone number _____

Choir Practice Time

Always keep the rehearsals moving. Begin with prayer and go right into some lively song the group knows, to get their voices warmed up and to get their attention. Use several selections in each practice session, with several three-minute breaks to let the singers talk and relax a little. During this time the director can have opportunity to talk with the accompanist. Do not let breaks get out of hand; but, rather, make sure that, at the end of the break, the choir gets back to business.

Be very, very businesslike in dealings with the teenagers during rehearsals. In recreational times, be one of them; love them, let them know that you can be young and that you want to be one of them. But in rehearsal, be businesslike, conveying to them the message that you are quite serious about the task at hand.

The Kind of Music

Music should be evangelistic, but music used with the teenage choir should differ slightly from music used with the adult choir. It should be very solid and heart-warming. Use some three-part harmony arrangements—sopranos and altos and a third part for the boys, a baritone part. Neither tenor nor bass, that part is not too high or too low for young changing voices, which are seldom either a low teenage bass or a very high tenor. Many music publishers produce teenage choir arrangements in three-part harmony, called SAB, soprano, alto and baritone. The teens like to use music with life and challenge in it, songs of Christian testimony, and songs that present the love of Christ. Have something new and fresh for them to work on at each rehearsal.

Discipline

The first rehearsal sets the pace for discipline. From the very beginning, let every teen know that, when the director comes into the rehearsal room, he runs the show. He is the boss; they must do what he says. Of course he must love them, and they must know that he does. They must realize that following his leadership is the only way the rehearsal can be successful and honor Christ.

When they do exceptionally well, compliment them. When the choir has a good rehearsal, let them know it was. If they do an excellent job in a service, make some public mention of it. Make them act as they ought. In this day and time teenagers find a great deal of security in being made to do right. They are seldom disciplined at home or at school; if at choir rehearsal they are made to do right, they feel security and a sense of belonging. Underneath definite authority, show a great deal of love. Teens must realize their interest and the work of Christ is near the director's heart.

Keep in Contact With the Members

Keep an accurate account of attendance at each rehearsal and use the phone and personal contacts to keep up with absentees. Remind them that they promised to be present for every rehearsal and performance. While this is not to be held over their heads, they are to realize at all times that they are bound by their application pledge.

Recruiting New Members

Be on the alert for teenagers in the church who need to be in the choir. An annual music survey will help discover prospects.

Provide Outside Singing Opportunities

Other churches have revival meetings and might be delighted to have a teenage choir to come one night to sing for them. Perhaps the teens can sing for a conference or youth rally. Outside singing opportunities provide an outlet other than the regular services, in which they can be of service to Christ.

Motivate Faithfulness

Try in the choir to instill a sense of faithfulness. This will help a great deal when they become adult choir members. Stress faithfulness often.

Train the Choir Musically

Take time in rehearsal to share the basic fundamentals of music. The public school system helps a great deal in this, but not all teens receive musical instruction in school.

Provide Some Recreation for Choir Members

This is especially needful if no other youth activities are provided by the church.

Chapter IX

Children's Choirs

The children should be divided into choirs according to grades. There are several reasons for having children's choirs. Many Primaries and Juniors are Christians and need a place of service to which they can give themselves and know they are serving Christ. There is something fresh and precious about a children's choir that adds greatly to the services. At the church where the writer serves, children's choirs take turns singing every third Wednesday night. They can be also used effectively in special Christmas, Thanksgiving, or Easter music programs.

Starting the Choirs

In starting the children's choirs, start big and recruit as rapidly as possible. At the first meetings make big plans. Juniors, Primaries, and Beginners like to be a part of the mass. Do not set the age limits too closely. Keep the age limits wide so that a maximum number of children may be in each choir. Have not less than three children's choirs, for the groups mentioned above. Since they are usually divided in that manner in Sunday school, they will resent any overlapping of the age span in the choirs. Juniors feel that they are much "bigger" than Primaries, and Primaries feel that Beginners are "babies"; therefore, it is better to separate them.

A good workable number for a Junior choir is fifty, while forty is about the maximum for Primaries. Twenty-five is tops for Beginners. When the choirs exceed these numbers, they should be divided. In Primary and Junior choirs separate boys and girls, when dividing, rather than ages. Juniors need an age span from the third to the sixth grade. The third and fourth graders give the volume needed, and the fifth and sixth graders lend a little more maturity and music knowledge to the group. Older juniors can sing parts readily.

People who have good rapport with children—and a keen imagination—should be used as directors for these choirs. Musical knowledge is just one qualification for the children's choir director. Their total qualifications should be considered carefully.

The church music director should keep in touch with younger choirs, making sure that they have needed materials and equipment, and proper space. He should help promote their attendance.

Each children's choir rehearsal should have a director and a pianist, plus two or three adult helpers, who will assist by (1) checking the roll; (2) helping to keep order; (3) getting the children ready to sing in a service; (4) planning and assisting at social events and parties; (5) transportation, and (6) passing out and collecting music sheets and books during rehearsals.

Music to Use

With Beginners use songs understood by and written for young children. They will sing meaningfully what is on their level. Primary and Junior choirs can use song arrangements, and will take pride in doing them well. Even some Primaries carry the alto part well. Do not be content with singing only choruses, but use choir arrangements. Several music publishers can supply these for children's choirs, and will send catalogs and/or samples upon request.

Make sure the children learn their parts correctly. They should not merely sing words but should be taught the meaning of the lyrics they sing. Help them to understand that they are to convey to the audience a message in song. Remember, many of them have already become Christians.

Social Activities

Have occasional parties or social activities with the children's choirs, but let these things work for you. Let the children know that these fun events are the reward for a job well done. A party or outing may be an award in an attendance drive, or for a good rehearsal or a good performance in a service.

Recruiting New Members

I have found that the awarding of a trophy helps a great deal in recruiting new members. We present a "Choir Member of the Year" trophy at the end of each choir year.

In Junior and Primary choirs two women keep attendance records. The contest runs all year (the choir year should correspond with the Sunday school year). At the end of the year, the choir member with the best attendance record, and who has also brought the greatest number of visitors or new members, gets the trophy. Points may be taken away for bad conduct. The trophy should be engraved "Choir Member of the Year," stating the year and the name of the choir, the church, and the pastor. Many choir members work hard to bring new members and to always be on time for rehearsals in order to win this trophy. The trophy is not small or insignificant; it is a nice, big, beautiful loving cup. It is usually presented to the winner in a Wednesday evening service.

Discipline

While extra sponsors help a great deal with the discipline in children's choirs, the choir director should maintain order in the choir. Juniors, especially, can get out of hand very rapidly. Let them know who is boss, but, again and again, let them know that they are loved.

In the children's rehearsals, especially in Beginner and Primary choirs, there should be periods of relaxation. The children should be able to get a drink or use the restroom, but should be closely supervised.

Training

Start with Primaries and Juniors to instill a sense of faithfulness to choir practice and to performance in the church services. These groups can understand also a great deal about music fundamentals. Many have already learned them in music classes at school. Using a chalkboard, draw the different notes, rests, sharps, flats, staffs, etc., and use them for drill in these basics.

If children learn some of these facts as Primaries, they will make much better Junior choir members. If they learn more as Juniors, they will make good Teenage choir members. And if they continue their training and accomplish more as Teenage choir members, they will make excellent Adult choir members. This is a strong point in favor of a graded choir program. The result, of course, is better choir members in every phase of the choir work.

Special Junior Ensembles

Often a Junior choir will be blessed with several children of exceptional talent. Small ensembles can be formed with these children, adding to the variety and effectiveness of the total music program.

A junior girls' trio, for example, in a Wednesday evening service, can add a brightness rarely achieved. From a musical standpoint their singing may not be overwhelming, but because their parents are in the congregation, and because they exhibit talent and musical confidence, their contribution will be enjoyed.

This specialized training and experience at an early age will be invaluable, in years to come, in forming teen or adult ensembles.

Choir Mothers

Mothers of many of the children in the choirs will be glad to help in the rehearsal time and in any other way they are needed. Use them as choir mothers and choir sponsors.

Chapter X

Music Fundamentals for Choir Members

Someone has said that music is a language understood by all mankind. How true this is. Many times we are moved by music when nothing else seems to touch our hearts.

Music—good music—is a gift from God and should be regarded as such. Only God can give man the beautiful melodies that we have today. Man has, in many cases, with his corrupt and evil mind, dragged music through the mire and caused some of it to be a thing of disgust and to be shunned by Christians. Yet on the other hand we still have God-given sacred music that should be regarded very highly.

Every song that we sing in church services should be sung with an air of reverence to God. Many of the songs that we have came as expressions of the hearts of men to God as they were moved by the Holy Spirit.

There is much said in the Bible concerning singing and praising God with song. A favorite Scripture text is Colossians 3:16, "Let the word of Christ dwell in you richly in all wisdom; teaching and admonishing one another in psalms and hymns and spiritual songs, singing with grace in your hearts to the Lord."

Music Fundamentals:

I. Main elements of music—all music falls into one of these three.
   A. Rhythm—This deals with the timing or lengths of tones and how often they occur.

B. Melody—This is the tune. (A continuation of tones one after another in a desired pattern.) All music is built around the melody.

C. Harmony—This is a combination of two or more tones sounded together that produce a pleasing effect.

II. A tone and its makeup—A tone is a sound with a definite pitch. This is caused by regular vibrations. A tone may be musical or nonmusical, not good or bad. A tone has four characteristics.

A. Length—long or short

B. Pitch—high or low

C. Power—loud or soft

D. Quality—sad, joyful, firm, etc.

III. The departments of music

A. Rhythmics—the lengths of tones

B. Melodies—the pitch of tones

C. Dynamics—the power and quality of tones

D. Theory—the principles and rules of music

IV. Notes and Rests

A. A note is a figure used to represent the length of a tone. Its position on the staff determines the pitch on the tone.

B. A rest is a figure used to represent the length of silence in a musical passage.

Notes are as follow:		Rests are as follow:	
A whole note	o	A whole rest	
A half note	♩	A half rest	
A quarter note	♪	A quarter rest	‰
An eighth note	♪	An eighth rest	⅞
A sixteenth note	♪	A sixteenth rest	⅞

A dot following the note gives the note its full value PLUS ½ of its value. For example: a ♩ gets 2 beats while a ♩. gets 3 beats.

V. A MUSIC STAFF consists of five parallel, horizontal lines and four spaces.

A line above or below the staff is a ledger line.

A score is one or more staves that run across the page and are joined by a vertical line called a brace.

There are three kinds of clefs.

1. Treble clef —ladies' voices

2. Bass clef —men's voices

3. Tenor clef —men's voices

Each staff is divided into measures by measure bars.

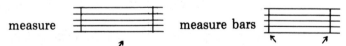

measure   measure bars

Each measure has an equal number of beats in it according to the rhythm of the song or selection of music.

VI. Division of Voices:
    1. Soprano—ladies—high voices
    2. Alto—ladies—low voices

  3. Tenor—men—high voices
  4. Bass—men—low voices
Women sing ONLY soprano and alto. Men ONLY sing
tenor and bass.

VII. Time signatures:

  At the beginning of each song is a TIME SIGNATURE
which tells how many beats are in each measure and which
note gets one beat.

Examples:

  The TOP number tells the number of beats in a measure,
and the LOWER number tells which note gets one beat.

Example: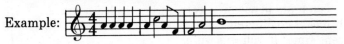

  Here there are four beats per measure and a quarter note
gets one beat.

VIII. Key signatures:

  At the beginning of each song there is a KEY
SIGNATURE which tells what key the song is in. It tells
which notes are to be lowered and which are to be raised
according to the key of the song.

  A flat (♭) lowers the note 1/2 step. A sharp (♯) raises
the tone a 1/2 step. A natural (♮) cancels any sharp or
flat.

  Major key signatures:

  C F B♭E♭ A♭ D♭ G D A   E   B

IX. The pattern for the major scale is as follows:

Chapter XI

The Mechanics of Proper Singing

The most important prerequisite to being a good choir member is to have a God-given desire to sing for His glory. An enthusiasm for the choir program is the single most vital factor in the success of the program.

Not every person will be able to sing as well as every other one. It makes no difference how poorly or how well you sing at the present time, if you are willing to approach the study with confidence and with pleasure and with a desire to serve Christ in this manner.

Someone has said, *"Music is often called the language of the emotions and furnishes greater personal satisfaction and pleasure than any other art form."*

The singing of Christians is found in all the Scriptures. Singing is a very natural expression; therefore, we should sing as spontaneously as we speak. Make up your mind, right now, that you are going to get rid of your inhibitions and try to eliminate tensions as much as possible so that you can sing freely, spontaneously, and with your whole soul.

Any person with a normal speaking voice, say many experts, can learn to sing. He should have an intense desire to work and to improve himself if he is going to sing, pleasingly. Of course, some people are born with a great deal more native ability, but others who are able to put forth a great effort can sing, also.

Fear is one of the greatest enemies of most singers. Of course, fear is greatly minimized in a choir situation, as opposed to singing as a soloist.

Any singer must have a very optimistic outlook. Consider, also, the following suggestions.

Breathing

Ninety per cent of good singing is good breathing. There are no magical tricks that ensure anyone of proper breath control. It requires hard work and good coaching.

Singers must learn diaphragmic breathing. The diaphragm is a large, dome-shaped muscle dividing the body between the lungs and abdomen. It is the most important single muscle used.

One must learn to fill all of the lungs, even to the bottom recesses, and to conserve the flow of air.

To learn to breathe correctly one should stand very tall, with the shoulders high, and place the hands just above the waistline (as illustrated), and, with the breath, push the hands forward. If this is done correctly, you can feel the air moving into the lower part of the lungs. The chest should remain high at all times.

Another way to make sure that you are breathing correctly is to place your hands against your rib cage, next to your spine, as illustrated, and while breathing feel the hands expand. Strive to expand the rib cage as much as possible.

While singing, try to let as little air escape as possible during each word. If the muscles around the waistline are not kept steady the control will completely collapse. Some call this "relaxation verses tension." There should be a feeling of firmness, but not rigidity in the lower abdominal walls at all times.

Each time a breath is taken the lungs should be filled to capacity. This can be done very quickly after a little practice.

Diction

The proper pronunciation of words is essential in choral music. The scriptural message is very important. If the audience is not able to ascertain that message because of poor diction or enunciation then the lesson is lost.

Colossians 3:16 states, *"Let the word of Christ dwell in you richly in all wisdom; teaching and admonishing one another in psalms and hymns and spiritual songs, singing with grace in your*

Illustration No. 1

Illustration No. 2

Illustration No. 4

Illustration No. 3

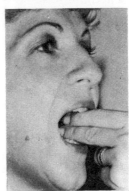

Illustration No. 5

hearts to the Lord.'' If we are going to teach, they must understand what we are singing.

A good definition of singing is "elongated, intensified speech." Of course, only the vowels are elongated. The consonants seem to have the job of connecting the vowel sounds.

It must be kept in mind that the lips and the tip of the tongue are the most vital areas of the mouth in the proper pronunciation of words. Lynn A. Christi, in his book, *Expressive Singing,* has this advice on diction:

> (1) Sing as naturally and spontaneously as you speak. (2) Practice reading poetry and drama until you are an excellent dramatic reader. (3) The standard pronunciation of words is indicated in a good dictionary and should be followed unless you are singing a dialect song. (4) Discover and correct as soon as possible any incorrect pronunciations or speech inadequacies. (5) Before singing any song, first read the text aloud, analyzing the meaning, mood, and word accent or emphases. (6) When singing, always aim at telling the story to the audience: make your text both eloquent and easily understood.

Posture

The correct singing posture is very easy to develop. One simply has to place his heels, hips, shoulders, and head against a wall and walk away keeping the shoulders very high and the head erect. See illustration number three.

Another way to position yourself is to lift the arms as high over the head as is possible and then lower them, letting the arms swivel at the shoulders. When the arms have returned to your side you are in the correct singing position.

Most choirs perform while standing; therefore, standing positions have been illustrated first. Since a great deal of practicing is done sitting down a certain amount of effort should be made to maintain a good posture while seated. The body from the hips up should be in much the same position as when standing. See illustration number four.

Always keep the chest raised comfortably high before you inhale and remain in this position as much as is possible to the end of a phrase or the entire song. The best way to maintain a good posture, whether seated or standing, is to concentrate on the high chest position. This gives you a feeling of stretching the spine.

Sometimes concentration on the shoulders will keep the chest in a high position. The shoulders should always be level and relaxed. They should not be rigid or slumped in any way or at any time.

The head is very important also. Many times singers have a tendency to reach for high notes with the chin. When you realize the high notes are coming soon, consciously lower the chin and tuck it in slightly. This causes the neck and throat muscles to relax and pushes the tone higher into the roof of the mouth, giving a more pleasing sound.

Rhythm

Rhythm seems to be one of the most difficult areas in choral music. All choirs, at times, have problems with it.

You will find that you are less apt to depend on others if you develop a strong rhythmic response to music. There is no better way to solve this problem than to count "1,2,3,4" according to the time signature. The time signature is explained in Chapter II, "Fundamentals of Conducting." Practice by tapping your foot while reading the song aloud, in correct rhythm, all the way through.

The choir should strive, under the director, to master the rhythmic patterns suggested in each song or choir arrangement. More choirs have problems with the dotted eighth, followed by a sixteenth note, than any other combination of notes.

Another common problem is the sustaining of tones to the end of the note value, especially at the ends of phrases where you might have a whole note or two whole notes tied together.

Nothing is more distracting to an audience than for a choir to pay little or no attention to the rhythmic pattern. Make sure you conquer this problem.

Tone Production

Before any singer can produce a pleasing tone he must have

some concept of what a beautiful tone sounds like. Some are blessed with more pleasing voices than others. Those who do not have good quality voices should listen very carefully to outstanding singers and in some cases perhaps emulate the tones. The tones that you sing should have a great deal of vitality and ring to them; the soft as well as the loud tones.

Good tone quality comes from a great deal of attention being paid to the vowel sounds. Make sure that you sing free and with an open throat keeping the teeth as widely apart as possible. This gives resonance.

The teeth are very important in singing. Place two fingers in your mouth as shown in the illustration and sing a phrase, forcing the teeth to remain open. That exercise will give you some idea of the difficulty of keeping the teeth open, but will, if practiced, help you to blend more readily with other choir members if they are paying close attention to the same type of tone production.

Vibrato, or an oscillation of the voice around the pitch, gives a beautiful tone production. A pleasing vibrato is imperative when singing any solo parts. Any voice that is free and without restriction will have its own natural vibrato. A straight tone has no fluctuation and the vocal cords are very tight and tense. One should never try to effect a vibrato in his voice, but when he becomes relaxed and sings freely then a natural vibrato will appear.

Every singer should strive for a basic feeling of resonance and vibration behind the eyes and nose. This sensation is realized when the tone is produced in the relaxed upper part of the throat. The tone then goes through the head and proceeds up into the roof of the mouth and then down and out through the teeth producing a vibration in the nose and cheekbone.

This may sound very strange to you now, but the more experience you gain in proper singing the more it will become a reality to you and the more pleasing your voice will be to others.

Stage Deportment

Realize at all times that you are on display in the choir loft. That, of course, is not your reason for being there; it's just a reality. Make sure that your dress and your attitude are suitable to the occasion at all times.

Memorize the Songs

Many directors agree that "memorizing" a song and "learning" a song are much the same thing. The message of the music is so important that the lyrics should be read slowly and thoughtfully, making sure that the message sinks deep into the heart of each choir member. The ensuing desire to propagate this message then causes memorization to become more rapid.

Discovering the idea or message in each sentence will soon become a basis for memorization. Paying close attention to the rhythm of the phrases in the lyrics, also, helps in memorizing.

Chapter XII

Fundamentals of Conducting

Every volunteer choir member should have some knowledge of the conductor's procedures which includes the downbeat, the cutoff and the patterns used for the various time signatures. Musical selections are written in various time patterns and the choir member should understand the hand motions used by the director.

Each choir director might vary these patterns, but they are generally universally the same.

Time and space do not permit, nor is it essential to go into an exhaustive study of conducting, but a few fundamentals are necessary.

There may be times when you need to lead songs for a Sunday school class or some such gathering. Why not have some knowledge of the procedure?

The following diagrams will show the motions of the hand for beating time in the different kinds of measure:

I. Double measure, 2/2, 2/4, 2/8, is the smallest and most simple of all measures. It has two beats.

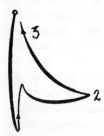

The first is downward and accented, the second is upward and unaccented. The first beat should be given straight downward with flexible arm and shoulder. When this beat is delivered properly the hand moves from the starting position and descends to the waistline. Every downward beat rebounds slightly to the right before proceeding into the second beat. The rebound must be made in a way that will not be confusing with the regular beat. After the rebound the upward beat is a little to the left, but never to the right. All downward beats are made a little to the right of the body, and never in front of the body.

Stand erect! Lift the hand slightly above the head. Now bring the arm down as far as the waist with a rebound and upward swing for the second beat. Repeat several times. Study diagram and practice before a mirror. Apply these instructions in double measure to the songs, "Jesus Loves Me" and "Joy to the World!" Sing as you beat the measure.

II. Triple measure, 3/2, 3/4, 3/8, has three beats, the first strong and the second and third weak. The motions of the hand for beating time in this measure are *down*, right, up. The first beat in all measures is the same as that described in double measure. The second beat begins with the rebound from the first, which carries the arm in a curving motion to the right. The third beat is curved upward as seen in the diagram, and brings the arm into position for the first beat of the next measure.

Practice "Faith of Our Fathers" and "America." Use the mirror.

III. Quadruple measure, 4/2, 4/4, 4/8, has four beats, the first strong, the second weak, the third medium, and the fourth weak. Beating time for this measure is *down*, left, *right*, up. Follow the diagram. Study such songs as "My Faith Looks Up to Thee," "Shall We Gather at the River?" and "What a Friend We Have in Jesus."

Use the mirror and study your direction form.

IV. Sextuple measure, 6/4, 6/8, has six beats; the first and fourth accented. The motions for beating this measure are *down*, left, left, *right*, up, up. Long beat downward, two short beats to the left, one long beat to the right, two short beats upward. This measure is also called compound double measure.

When leading songs of fast tempo or compound double, two beats are made as a double measure—1, 2, and 3 on the downward beat, and 4, 5, and 6 on the upward beat. Sextuple measure is given six beats only when the movement is slow. Use for six-beat songs, "Day Is Dying in the West" and "Near the Cross." Follow Sextuple diagram. For two-beat songs, use "Jesus Is Calling" and "There Shall Be Showers of Blessing." Follow double measure diagram. Practice before the mirror.

V. Miscellaneous Patterns. Other less used compound measures are: Compound triple, 9/4, 9/8, and compound quadruple, 12/4, 12/8. In congregational leading the nine beats in compound triple measure are reduced to three beats as in triple measure. The motion for beating this measure is *down*, right, up as in triple measure. Follow triple measure diagram and practice "Blessed Assurance" and "I Must Tell Jesus." The twelve beats in compound quadruple measure are reduced to four as in quadruple measure. The motion for beating this measure is *down*, left, right, up. Follow quadruple measure diagram. Use such songs as "Saved, Saved" and "More Holiness Give Me."

Many songs, such as "How Firm a Foundation," "O Happy Day," "Stand Up, Stand Up for Jesus," "Just as I am," "Blessed Assurance," and "Saved, Saved" begin on some beat other than the first of the measure. If the song begins with the last beat, the initial stroke will be upward. Practice many songs in all measures.

A hold (fermata) on any beat in the measure is indicated by bringing the hand to the position of attention. The release of a hold, phrase, or at the end of a composition is indicated by a "cutoff" sign after the note is held its allotted time.

Some objectives:

(1) Learn to recognize time signatures and what patterns should be used.

(2) Accept opportunities to lead singing. You can be a better follower if you do.

(3) Learn to follow carefully the patterns of the choir director.

(4) Look for opportunities to further your training.

VI. WATCHING THE DIRECTOR. Watching the director is of the utmost importance. It is mentioned elsewhere in this book, but it cannot be stressed too greatly.

It is very necessary that the choir members keep eye contact with the conductor as much as possible. A director can communicate with facial expressions more than with any other method.

Chapter XIII

The Soloist

Often members of the choir step forward and sing solo parts or present a special number as a soloist, thus becoming an individual performer with a greater responsibility. Therefore, the following is deemed very necessary and helpful to individuals blessed with the ability to sing alone.

In most evangelistic church services a part of the music program is the singing of at least one soloist. There are two main reasons for this: (1) people everywhere love to hear a single voice, and (2) it is much easier to have a soloist to sing than to combine voices in special ensembles. I am not advocating that a great number of soloists should be used; I am simply stating that a number are used in the average church.

A special solo number is usually performed just before the message. It is thought that perhaps a single voice can prepare the hearts of the people for the message more readily than a choir or an ensemble. Keeping in mind that a solo, tastefully rendered, can contribute greatly to an evangelistic service, there are some special aspects that should be considered.

The Testimony and Christian Experience of the Soloist

Any soloist who stands before a congregation to sing a message of Christ should have assurance that he has been born again. There should have been a time in his life when he realized that he was lost and yielded his heart and life to Jesus Christ. Many churches have paid soloists who are considered only for their beautiful voices and their musical renditions, with no mention made of their spiritual experience. They sing from the intellect and not from the heart. Again, the singer should be saved and mean sincerely the message he is singing.

The Musical Background of the Soloist

Many singers are born with a good "instrument" and can do an acceptable job as a soloist without formal training. For this wonderful gift any singer should be truly thankful. A soloist can better equip himself if he can find a good teacher and take some voice training. There are some basics that are essential to good singing.

It is good for a singer to be able to read music so that he can learn new material quickly, or so that he can thumb through a hymnal or songbook and pick out beautiful songs. It is also a definite advantage for a soloist to have the proper breathing technique. Ninety per cent of good singing is proper breathing. More will be said in this chapter concerning breathing.

I have been a soloist for approximately twenty-three years. It was not until my second year at college that I decided to study music seriously. After my first voice lesson, I asked my teacher, "Will I ever be able to sing a solo?" Her reply was, "If you are willing to work very long and very hard, you might one day be able to sing a solo, perhaps." I determined that I would work long and hard and accomplish this for Christ. The results were that I studied voice for approximately six years, five years under Donella Brown, at Tennessee Temple College. I practiced one song for three years before performing it in public—"The Lord's Prayer," by Mallott.

There is absolutely no short cut to becoming a good vocalist. It takes about five or six years for a young singer's abdominal muscles to position and harden so that he can rely on them to help him with breathing and breath control. The only reason that many singer cannot sing into their sixties and seventies is that they loose breath control. Any singer who slacks off and does not continue these exercises will diminish in his ability to sing well.

Any singer who has not had training should avail himself of a voice coach or teacher to help him with these basic exercises. Every Christian singer should strive to be his best. One need not be second-rate just because he believes the Bible.

The Choice of a Song

The soloist's choice of the right song is of utmost importance to the service. Several things should be considered in choosing a song:

1. *Type of Service.* In an evangelistic service where reaching the lost is the primary goal the soloist should choose a song with a testimony or salvation message. All too often, soloists choose songs that are particularly suited to their voices, but are lacking in the really scriptural message needed for the occasion.

Some singers have what they call "sugar stick" songs that they have done many times before. These should be used very prayerfully in soul-winning services.

Songs of a general nature should be used for other than soul-winning services. They should be chosen carefully, but more variety is allowed in other services.

2. *Variety.* All soloists should try to learn a variety of songs so that their repertoire might be enlarged, enabling them to sing the proper selections on many different occasions.

3. *New Songs.* All soloists should be constantly searching for new songs. Homer Britton suggested to me in the summer of 1953, "Learn at least one new song every day." This practice would add an amazing variety and depth to any singer's storehouse of material.

The Choice of a Soloist

The music director should consult with the pastor before choosing persons as soloists for church services. Just as the members of the different ensembles should be chosen in consultation with the pastor, the soloists should have his approval. Often, because of personal counseling, the pastor will have certain information concerning an individual that is not known to the music director. This information could allow him to better choose and select persons who should appear on the church platform.

Chapter XIV

Musical Terms Every Choir Member Should Know

Musical terms are sometimes difficult to understand by trained musicians. Most of them are in the Italian language. The following are the most often used musical terms along with their definitions. Volunteer choir members should become acquainted with them. They save time in the rehearsals and keep the choir on the same track. They are as follows:

A cappella—Vocal music unaccompanied.

Accelerando—Gradually increasing the rate of speed.

Accent—Emphasis upon a certain tone, chord, or beat.

Accidentals—All signs for raising or depressing notes that are not found in the signature.

Allegretto—A little slower than allegro.

Alto—Originally applied to high male voices, now generally to the lowest female voice.

Andante—Movement in moderate time.

A tempo—In time.

Attack—A firm entry of voices or instruments at a leading point.

Bar, double—Heavy double lines drawn vertically through the staff, dividing off different parts or designating the end of a composition. Dots placed on either side of a double bar mean that preceding or following measures are to be repeated.

Bass Clef—The F clef on the fourth line.

Brace—A mark connecting two or more staves together.

Cantata—A short work in the musical form of an oratorio.

Choral—For a chorus or choir.

Chord—A combination of musical sounds, consonant and dissonant.

Chorus—A body of singers. The refrain of a song. A composition for a body of singers.

Clef—The sign set at the head of the staff to fix the pitch or position of one note, and thus of the rest.

D—(1) The second note of the normal scale C. (2) the scale having two sharps in its signature. (3) The name given to a string tuned to D. The third string of the violin and second of the viola and cello.

Decrescendo—To decrease in volume of sound.

Descant, discant—Treble or soprano voice; addition of a part or parts to a tenor or subject.

Dot—A dot set after a note prolongs its time value by half; a second or third dot prolongs the time value of the dot immediately preceding it by half.

Double bar—The two vertical lines drawn through the staff at the end of a section, movement, or portion to be repeated.

Falsetto—The artificial tones of the voice, higher than the chest or natural voice.

Fermata—A pause.

Fine—The end. Used to show the end of a piece or movement, after a repeat, or partial repeat.

Flat—The character which lowers the pitch of the note a semitone.

Forte—Loud, strong; usually written *f*.

Fortissimo—Extremely loud (usually written *ff*).

Grace-note—An ornamental note, written small, with an oblique line through the stem.

Harmony—The agreement or consonance of two or more simultaneous tones. The art of combining tones into chords and treating those chords in a rational manner.

Hold—A character indicating that the time of a note or rest is to be prolonged.

Improvise—To create on the spur of the moment.

Interlude—A short piece played between longer musical sections, acts or services.

Interval—The difference in pitch between two simultaneous tones.

Introduction—A phrase or division preliminary to and preparatory of a composition or movement.

Key—(1) The series of tones forming any given major or minor scale. The signature of a given major key also serves for its relative minor key. (2) A finger or foot-lever for producing tone in a piano or organ.

Largo—Very slow, broadly.

Larynx—The organ of the voice, by which we produce vocal sounds, situated at the top of the windpipe.

Legato—In a smooth, connected manner.

Melody—A succession of tones, rhythmically and symmetrically arranged to produce a pleasing effect.

Moderato—Moderately.

Monotone—Unvarying tone.

Note—A sign which, by its form, shows us the relative duration of a sound, and by its position on the staff the pitch of a sound.

Obbligato—An additional part to a vocal or instrumental solo.

Octave—Eight notes above or below, the interval of an eighth.

Phrase—Part of a nausical sentence.

Piano—Softy, abbd. p.

Postlude—A closing voluntary on the organ.

Presto—Rapidly; faster than allegro.

Refrain—The chorus at the end of every stanza of some songs.

Rests—Signs indicating silence of the same duration as the notes for which they stand.

Run—A rapid succession of notes.

Scale—A series of consecutive tones proceeding by half steps (chromatic) or by half steps, whole steps, with occasional step and a half (Major, minor, whole tone, pentatonic)

Score—Copy of a musical work, of which the parts are written on separate staves, placed under each other.

Sign—A note or character employed in music.

Slur—A curved line placed over notes directing that they be sung legato. Used also in modern music to indicate phrasing.

Staccato—In a crisp detached manner.

Tempo—Time. "Tempo" is universally used to mean "rate of movement."

Treble—The highest voice or part; also Treble or G clef.

Vibrato—A tremulous quality of tone.

Vocal—Belonging to the voice; music intended to be sung.

Vocalize—Vocal exercises.

Volume—Quantity of tone.

Well-tempered—Satisfactory pitch relationship.

Whole rest—A pause equal in time to a whole note.

Chapter XV

Music and the Church Budget

A good church music program costs money, a lot of money. Some churches think that whatever the music program costs, it is inexpensive compared to the tremendous results. When the church decides that they are willing to make some expenditures for the music program, the program is on its way to becoming an integral part of the church ministry.

For too many years, the average church member has felt that the music program is something "scratched together" on Sunday morning, with little preparation, and that it operates at no cost other than the price of the piano or the organ. Pianos, organs, and music supplies have, as have all commodities, experienced inflation. It takes more money now than it did a few years ago to have a good music program.

If, in fact, the music budget is planned, it must deal with several questions.

Why Have a Music Budget?

The Scriptures exhort that all things should be done decently and in order. The word "all" is inclusive and covers the music program. If money is going to be spent on the music program, it should be spent in an orderly manner with a budget. The music director or someone in charge should help to determine how much is actually needed for music over a twelve-month period. If a budget is being drawn up for the first time, then wise counsel should be sought from pastors and music directors who have done such planning for several years.

A budget will force a choir director to plan his music expenditures and be able to give reasons for the purchases. No music director should be given unlimited purchasing power, because this is a temptation to overspend and waste God's money. Every human being needs to answer to somebody for his actions; therefore, a budget insures that the music director or the purchasing agent for the music department will exercise proper caution in spending the money.

A church budget will keep the expenditures for music in line with expenditures for other things in the music program. While it is sad to spend an excessive amount, it is even sadder to take shortcuts and cause the total church program to suffer.

What Does the Money Buy?

1. Sheet music is a valid category for the music budget. Most good, new compositions are published in sheet-music form, and three copies of a single title (one for the soloist, one for the organist, and one for the pianist) will cost about $4.50, as opposed to $1.50 a few years ago. In the course of a year, it is easy to see what 45 or 50 selections would cost.

2. Collections of choir arrangements range in price from $1.95 to $2.95. The number of selections in a book will vary from eight to fifteen or twenty. The books with a larger number of selections are usually more expensive, with more pages but, in some cases, simpler arrangements. By adding one collection of choir arrangements every month or two, quite a volume of choir music can be collected over a year's time.

These books have a way of disappearing, I might add, and should be carefully dispensed by the choir librarian.

3. The tuning and repair of pianos and organs are budget expenses. All pianos, no matter how expensive or inexpensive, get out of tune—new pianos more quickly than older ones. Environment has a great deal to do with the piano's ability to stay in tune. Continual changes of temperature cause the piano to need tuning often. Air conditioners play a major role in these changes.

Tuning of pianos costs more in recent years, so that a large church with several pianos can have a sizable tuning and repair bill; therefore, these costs need to be covered in the church music budget.

4. Music folders are needed for the choir. The best music folder this writer has found can be obtained from the Clamp Back Organization in North Hopkins, Minnesota. Some choirs have a performance folder and a rehearsal folder. These not only look good in the services but save a considerable amount of time in the practice sessions.

5. Files for choir music are needed. There are many different kinds of choir music files—some for the octavo size and some for the regular 8½ x 11 music. The number of files needed depends on the amount of sheet music used, so, this expense may vary.

6. Single choir arrangements are a good investment. Many companies now publish single arrangements from choir collections; these may be purchased at prices from about 30 to 55 cents per copy.

7. Robes or special clothing may be a budget item. New robes for a choir are not always needed but may be worked into the annual budget. Many choirs dress the ladies in matching dresses and the men in matching ties and blazers, as opposed to robes. Often these special outfits are worn only on special occasions. These are not usually in the church budget but are paid for by the choir members. At least one choir—the Adult Choir of the Northside Baptist Church, in Charlotte, North Carolina, that I presently direct—collects monthly gifts from each choir member for the purpose of buying special clothing.

A great deal of money can be saved by buying robe "kits" that can be sewn together by the ladies of the church. They are precut and have all of the incidentals with them, so that the whole job can be completed by anyone who has some knowledge of sewing. This project can be pursued with considerable savings to the church.

8. Revivals and conferences have some music expense but this can be covered by the offering during the meetings.

9. Miscellaneous expenses can include: (1) chorus sheets and songbooks for Sunday school departments; (2) music staff sten-

cils for duplicating; (3) flash cards and other visual aids for music training during the choir rehearsals.

How Are Budget Amounts Determined?

The vision of some churches is greater than others, and they would therefore use more money for the music program. But there is a rule of thumb that can be used by most churches to determine an equitable and fair amount for the music budget. When a church has a budget of $50,000 annually or less, music expenditures need to be kept small. A smaller church needs to keep a good music program going as well as a larger church, but it is much more difficult for smaller churches to have the financial liberty to pursue a large music program.

With $50,000 or above as annual figures, sizable amounts of money can be taken without damaging the total effectiveness of the church. This writer feels that of an annual church budget of that amount or larger, one per cent of the total should be spent each year on the music program. Of course, that would not include major expenditures such as salaries or the purchase of large equipment such as pianos.

How Can a Church Conserve Expenditures?

Every music director should consider himself a dedicated servant of Christ and realize that the music budget comes from offerings given by the rank and file of the church membership, the tithes and offerings of children, teenagers, and adults. This money should be used wisely and prayerfully, so that the maximum effectiveness can be gained from a minimum amount of financial expenditure.

This means that, occasionally, the director will make his own choir arrangement of a song instead of buying a collection of choir arrangements. This also means that the music director will supervise those working with him in the music program (accompanists and children's choir workers), and guide their purchases of music and materials, to be sure that the funds are conserved as much as possible.

Chapter XVI

Discovering Prospects

"What is the music potential of my church?" The answer to this question is important for every music director to know, and there *are* ways to find out. A churchwide music survey is the best way to determine exactly the music potential in the church. Consider five things concerning this music survey.

What the Survey Contains

On a following page is a copy of the music survey blank used annually at the churches were the writer is and has been the minister of music. It asks for enough information concerning each person who fills out one to help any music director determine the music potential of his church. The information asked for in the first section is of vital importance to the overall work of the church. (Parents of primary and beginner age children should fill out one for them.)

Why Should a Survey Be Taken?

First, it answers the inevitable question, "Who can I get to sing in the choir?" In five minutes on Sunday morning, the answers can be determined. Second, the survey also shows the musical training and background of prospects.

How to Take the Music Survey

Discuss it with the pastor. Before taking a music survey discuss it with the pastor, thoroughly. After getting his approval, the music director and the pastor should determine the date for and the procedure to be used in taking the survey.

Discuss it with the teachers and officers of the Sunday school. The pastor and the music director, on the determined date, meet with the Sunday school teachers and officers and discuss the intention of taking a churchwide music survey. It should be done the following Sunday after this meeting. Each teacher is given a survey blank and taught how to fill it out, so that they in turn can instruct their pupils the following Sunday morning.

Impress on the teachers the tremendous importance of the survey and urge them to have *every* person present fill out the blank. Those presently in the choir should fill out a blank, also, to show a spirit of complete cooperation and to give other important information asked for on the blank.

Take the survey during the Sunday school. The superintendents and the teachers take the survey blanks with them to the classes and departments on the following Sunday morning, and take about five minutes to have each person fill out the blank and return it. When the survey blanks are turned in with the regular Sunday school records, they are then given to the music director for processing.

How to Break Down the Music Survey

The music director should go through and divide the survey by departments, after which they are separated into two categories: (1) Choir prospects and (2) non-prospects. The names of the prospects should be given to the directors of each choir. (Many music directors have children's choir workers helping in the program.)

Other Uses of the Survey

The first section of the survey blanks may reveal some visitation prospects. (See the blank.) Also, there may be found some who have had experience in songleading. They may be used in Sunday school classes or departments. You will find some instrumentalists and those who have had voice training. All of this information will be extremely helpful in building a great music program.

Music Survey

"Let the word of Christ dwell in you richly in all wisdom; teaching and admonishing one another in psalms and hymns and spiritual songs, singing with grace in your hearts to the Lord." Colossians 3:16

NAME_____ BIRTH DATE_____ ADULT_____

ADDRESS_____ CITY_____ STATE_____ PHONE_____

ARE YOU A CHRISTIAN?_____ CHURCH MEMBER_____ WHERE?_____
TO WHICH SUNDAY SCHOOL CLASS OR DEPARTMENT DO YOU BELONG?
_____

* * *

ARE YOU PRESENTLY SINGING IN A CHOIR OF THE CHURCH?_____
WOULD YOU BE INTERESTED IN SINGING IN ONE OF THE CHOIRS OF THE CHURCH?_____
HAVE YOU BEEN IN A CHOIR BEFORE?_____ WHERE?_____
CHECK YOUR VOICE RANGE_____ HIGH VOICE_____ LOW VOICE
DO YOU PLAY A MUSICAL INSTRUMENT?_____ NAME THE INSTRUMENT_____
HAVE YOU EVER LED SINGING?_____
HAVE YOU HAD ANY TYPE OF MUSICAL TRAINING?_____ WHAT TYPE?_____
HOW LONG?_____

* * *

CHECK GROUP TO WHICH YOU BELONG

ADULT_____   TEENS _____   JUNIOR _____   PRIMARY _____   BEGINNER _____
(18-up)   (13-17)   (9-12)   (6-8)   (4-5)

*PARENTS SIGN FOR PRIMARIES AND BEGINNERS
—Remarks—

_____
_____

☐ I WILL NOT BE ABLE TO BE A REGULAR CHOIR MEMBER BUT I WOULD LIKE
☐ TO KNOW MORE ABOUT THE SUBSTITUTE PLAN.
☐ I POSSIBLY COULD BE A SUBSTITUTE.

Chapter XVII

Special Choirs and Small Ensembles

Several different kinds of special choirs and small ensembles can be used to add variety and interest to a service.

The Men's Chorus

A men's chorus can be used very effectively on Father's Day or for a big patriotic program or service. The singing of men is especially enjoyed by most everyone. Many feel there is nothing more beautiful or more soul-stirring than a forceful song by a men's chorus in four-part harmony. It rouses an audience. Most choirs have a built-in men's chorus. Actually, the men's section of the Adult choir can be used as a male chorus. Or they can be combined with some older teenagers from the Teen choir. Preparing such a group to sing takes time and extra effort on the part of the men and the director, but the result is worth the effort.

Usually, eight, twelve, or sixteen voices, with two, three or four voices on each part, make up this music group. Often a radio choir is composed of twelve to sixteen voices. The famous Sixteen Singing Men are extensively used because of their great ability, and because of the magnificent performances obtained when sixteen talented, well-trained men have spent time in rehearsals.

The Ladies' Choir

A ladies' chorus is especially appropriate to use on Mother's Day or other similar occasions. Ladies singing in three and four-part harmony seem to have a very pleasing effect on any audience.

This can be a huge three-part chorus with several ladies singing first soprano, others the second-soprano part, and another group, alto. Ordinarily three-part harmony is used with this group, but occasionally four-part and five-part harmony can be very effective.

Small Ensembles

Besides adding brightness and variety to the church service not obtained in any other way, small ensembles allow large numbers of people to participate in the special music. The singers for triple trios, sextets, duets, quartets, trios, ladies' choruses, mixed quartets, and special smaller choirs should be carefully chosen, and should have regular weekly rehearsal periods.

When several ensembles are used alternately, the musical selections can be well rehearsed for a professional performance that will add dignity and sincerity to the services. In a church where this is true, a visitor may attend for a month and never hear the same group or soloist perform twice. It is impressive to visitors, and a great attraction to the church.

Kinds of Groups

1. *Trios.* Trios are usually made up of three female voices, although this is not imperative. The three female voices would be soprano, second soprano, and alto. A mixed trio could be soprano, alto, and tenor, or an alto, tenor, and baritone group could be most popular when well blended.

2. *Quartets.* These can be either men's, ladies', or mixed quartets. The most thrilling group to most church audiences is the male quartet, with a vibrancy and strength not found in ladies' or mixed quartets. Men's quartets are universal favorites.

3. *Sextets.* Some weaker or less-trained voices can be used in the ladies' group (soprano, second soprano and alto). Any treble arrangements can be used but a ladies' trio does best with trio arrangements.

The ladies' sextet has proven popular, possibly because it features six ladies, each of whom has friends in the congregation; but also, because of the group's size the rendition has a large, full sound.

Blend is relatively no problem in a ladies' sextet, though it might always be improved, if the right techniques are used. In any group each singer should listen to those standing next to her and, without going too far afield of right techniques, try to blend or imitate the tone of that person. Constant awareness of the need for a better blend will cause the group to "feel" together and blend more readily. As a general rule, any ensemble must sing together for a period of time before they begin to "feel" together and thus greatly improve their performances.

The standing arrangement of this (or any) ensemble is important. The physical appearance of the group should not take away from the message of the song. Still maintaining blend and balance, the taller persons should be placed on the outside and the shorter persons at the center, or vice versa.

4. *The Triple Trio.* This is, as the title suggests, a group of nine voices with three on each part. As with a sextet, other arrangements can be used, but this group is very effective when using regular trio arrangements. Three people singing each part achieve a confidence and security because each supports the other. Less-trained voices can participate if at least one good, strong, capable singer is the leader in each section of the triple trio.

The physical arrangement on the platform of a group this large needs careful planning. The approach to the platform should be worked out in rehearsal prior to the service time. For variety, use several different standing arrangements, other than a semicircle.

As a teen ensemble, six girls and three fellows may form a triple trio; with the young men singing the melody, three of the ladies singing second soprano, and the remaining three singing alto. Many fine three-part treble arrangements can also be used.

5. *The Octet.* While this ensemble can be a double men's quartet, it is usually a double mixed quartet. Range and degree

of quality depend on the talents of the individual singers. A carefully picked group may be able to do difficult arrangements not used by the choir with lesser trained voices.

6. *Miscellaneous.* There are other groups that can be used effectively to provide variety in a music program, such as a senior citizens' choir, an elderly ladies' chorus (over 65), or a deaf choir.

Choosing the Voices

Choose ensemble singers very, very carefully, well in advance of the actual enlisting. A good choir director should be able to know individual voices before making selections for a particular group. It is difficult to remove a person chosen for a group, if he or she does not work into the group adequately. Therefore, great care in selection should be used.

In a regular choir rehearsal, ensemble possibilities may be asked to sing a special portion of the arrangement. The director can obtain some idea of the quality and blendability of their voices. These singers may be chosen at random to sing these parts. In this way, a quartet or trio may be put together without the participants being aware that they are auditioning for a part in a special ensemble.

The Rehearsal Times

Each group should have its own practice time every week. If available, a captain or leader assigned to the group should meet with them, as well as an accompanist. They should be told well in advance of their next performance, so they can have their song so well rehearsed that their preparation will be evident.

Many times it is effective to designate one evening a week as music night at the church. The choir will rehearse; before or after choir practice, several groups may also have their rehearsals. This keeps people from having to spend too many nights away from their families. Also, some rehearsals may be scheduled before or after regular services; after the Wednesday evening service is a good time to practice.

Strict adherence to rehearsal times is of the utmost importance. It requires a great deal of discipline on the part of the director and the members, but it will pay off in quality music program that will bless the members of the church and add to the variety and effectiveness of the services.

At each practice rehearse at least three or four numbers. The major part of the rehearsal could be spent on the number to be performed next, and lesser amounts of time on other numbers for future performances. One or two numbers should be kept in readiness at all times so that a given group might be called on in an emergency if deemed necessary by the director. Numbers performed well in the services should be reviewed often, and repeated occasionally. It is a pity for a group to spend hours in rehearsal, perform a number that is evidently a blessing and help to the congregation, and then put it on a shelf and never use it again.

Performances

Because these special groups perform on the preaching platform before the whole congregation each individual should be approved by the pastor.

Each group should approach the platform in a professional manner, not slovenly or slipshod, but with eager anticipation of an opportunity to do a good job for Christ and be a blessing to the people. It should anticipate presenting a salvation message to the lost, or a Christian testimony to all. Good posture should be maintained at all times. Emphasis should be placed on this during rehearsals.

Wearing apparel should be modest and in good taste; many directors choose to have ensembles dress uniformly. This is very effective and gives the audiences an impression of the group's care and pride in its presentation.

The microphone placement should be practiced well in advance so that each singer knows exactly which mike he is to face. The control engineer for the PA system should be briefed, also.

Never should the performances be showy or the performers display an attitude of cockiness. They should be delighted and have a pleasantness that says, "We are here to do a job and to do it correctly for the Saviour."

Material to Use

A great variety of music can be obtained for special ensembles. Some groups are at home with music with a definite rhythmic pattern, while others like materials with expression and a variety of interpretation. All materials should contain a Christian, biblical message.

All music should be approved by the music director—if for no other reason, to keep two groups from working on the same number at the same time.

Record Keeping

Records should be kept of each ensemble, the dates of their performances, the songs they have sung, and copies of the arrangements. This, of course, will require the time of a choir secretary and a good filing system.

Chapter XVIII

The Pastor and the Music Program

Every pastor has a definite role to play if his music program is to be successful. Too often pastors have the attitude, "Oh, well, I'll just leave the music up to the music director; he knows more about that than I do." As far as the technical end of the music program is concerned, this may be true; but every pastor should know more about what his people need, in the way of music, than anyone else. He does not have to be a musician, but every pastor should know enough about the musical needs of his congregation to help guide the music program.

The Bible indicates that God gives each pastor a special gift; he has not promised this gift to the music director. The music director does not know the real spiritual needs of a congregation, therefore, he should depend on the pastor to give some direction in the music ministry. The pastor shouldn't plan in detail every aspect of the music program, but he is to provide the leadership in this area, as in others.

Two specific areas that need to be explored are discussed in this chapter.

The Pastor and the Music Director

Although many churches "call" the music director in much the same way as they do the pastor, the two are by no means partners. The pastor should have complete authority over the church and music director. The music director should recognize this. It is biblical. Hebrews, chapter thirteen, is the basis for this viewpoint. Any music director who does not recognize the authority and position of the pastor is heading for serious trouble, and perhaps will cause severe difficulties. The pastor should not tolerate insubordination on the part of any staff member. This is not to say that the pastor is the more favored in the sight of the Lord, or better than the music director, but God has His plan, and His plan is for the pastor to lead the church and the people. The music director is part of the church and the people. May God have mercy on a music director who takes it upon himself to try to lead the people away from the pastor, dividing the church.

The loyalty of a music director to his pastor should be without question. Any criticism or casting of a shadow on some decision or act of the pastor by the music director is unthinkable. In fact, the music director should not even listen to other church members who belittle or criticize the pastor in any way. He should actively defend the pastor at all times. If he cannot do this, he should quietly and quickly resign and move to another location.

On the other hand, any rumor about, or criticism of, the music director should be discounted by the pastor until proven. The pastor should defend the music director at all times, and especially in the face of criticism or belittlement. Each should pray daily for the other.

Mutual Support in the Public Services

There should be a visible spirit of cooperation. This puts the audience at ease, and makes for harmony and a good spirit in the services.

Quite often the pastor will have occasion to refer to the music director in his sermon. This should be done in good taste—and should be received well on the part of the music director. This endears both men to the audience.

The music director should deliberately recognize the authority of the pastor in the services, and should cause the music to fit the personality of the pastor. The messages of a young, energetic preacher calls for a music program in keeping with the active pastor. (In some cases, a more subdued program might give a much needed change of pace.) On the other hand, if a pastor is prone to be reserved or quiet, a more lively song service and music program might balance the service.

In summary, each should do all in his power to enhance the ministry of the other.

Choosing a Full-Time Music Director

1. *Finding a Candidate.* Possibly one of the most wide-open fields in Christianity today is that of the full-time music director. Most pastors and churches are looking for a "fancy Dan," who knows music but has no compassion for the lost or concern about being a real spiritual help to the church. Hundreds of churches across America need a good full-time music director who really wants to do a good job for the Saviour. Real soul-winning music directors are the crying need.

Many churches have a personnel committee. Perhaps this committee is fine when it comes to hiring janitors or secretaries, but the hiring of a full-time music director should be led by the pastor. He is in a better position to find out who is available in this field. Because the music director plays such an important role in the service of the church, his selection must be kept upon a high spiritual plane.

To any church, the choosing of a good music director is second in importance only to the choosing of a good pastor. This is another reason why the pastor should lead in this selection. As a general rule, it is best to consider someone already serving well in a church, unless a candidate who is just graduating from college or seminary is available.

The author does not advocate deliberately pulling a music director away from another church, but many times a music director may feel that a change is of the Lord, although he is doing a good job at the church he is presently serving. Every good music director, it seems, is busy somewhere.

Smaller churches might do well to carefully consider an undergraduate of a good Christian school, who is being trained, and who needs practical experience, in this field to prepare him for future success. He can gain this training while still in school, coming to the church on the weekends or during the summer.

The most important aspect in finding a good music director is the leading of the Lord. Every church should pray diligently that God would direct them in choosing the right man for them. Too many churches have had severe trouble because they were lax in choosing the right music director. Considering this and the other points set down, it is evident that the pastor must lead in this important selection.

2. *Interviewing the Candidate.* After a likely candidate has been found, then the pastor, not the personnel committee, should interview the candidate first. They may want to talk to him, and the deacons may want to interview or question him, but the pastor should make the first contact and have the first interview with the candidate. This can be done either by telephone or in person; but a personal interview is most desirable in every case.

Many questions can be answered to the satisfaction of both candidate and pastor at this first conference. First impressions are not always absolutely correct, but, many times, good rapport can be started at this point.

In this interview the pastor can obtain information about the candidate's training and personal background. Every music director should live in such a way that he would not fear to have his background explored by any committee or pastor of a church to which he may go. The pastor can, in the initial interview, acquaint the candidate with the kind of music program that he wants for his church, giving the candidate the opportunity to proceed or to gracefully back out, saving time and expense later on.

3. *Having the Candidate Visit the Church.* During the second or third interview, the prospective music director should be invited to visit the church, on a weekend, so that he may spend time in rehearsal with the choir, and may direct the music during one or both Sunday services. This does not give the congregation adequate knowledge of his ability to direct the complete music program, but it does give them some exposure to him, and he to them. Although his past record will be the deciding factor, the visit to the church is invaluable.

4. *Understanding Policies and Duties.* One of the most predominant difficulties experienced by music directors is the lack of a clear understanding of the policies of the pastor or the church, and of his duties. Often music directors have more than one duty to perform, especially in smaller churches. The music director might also take care of the religious education. Many times his title is Director of Music and Education, or Director of Music and Youth. Occasionally, the music director is considered as assistant pastor, or assistant to the pastor.

These dual titles or dual jobs are all the more reason for a definite understanding of the policies and duties before a music director takes a position in any church. Misunderstandings come about because of a lack in this area. This is not to say that everything must be put down in black and white, although that would not be wrong or out of place, but there should be a "gentlemen's agreement" or clear understanding of the exact duties and circumstances under which he must work. This can be taken care of in interview prior to his coming.

Choosing a Part-Time Music Director

1. *Finding a Candidate.* Most small churches are not financially able to hire a full-time director, or even a combination music and education director, or music and youth director. They may have to resort to hiring a member of the church as a part-time music director, or perhaps a student from a nearby college. The part-time music director does not have to be hired, but may be a volunteer from the congregation. Many good men in other professions are good musicians and have been trained to some extent in this field.

Although musical ability should be considered and given high priority, it is not the main consideration. The foremost prerequisite should be a dedicated Christian life and a desire to serve the church in a sincere manner. His loyalty to the pastor should be without question.

Desirable characteristics of a music director, full or part-time, will be discussed in a later chapter.

2. *Making Sure of Ability.* Any person being considered as part-time music director should be carefully scrutinized as to his musical ability. If the pastor is not adept or proficient in music himself, he should get counsel from reliable members of the church as to the abilities of a possible candidate. A personable, good, sincere man within the church who knows very little about music would not be a good candidate for the job of part-time music director. The prime qualification, beyond that of sincere Christian attitude, is good musical ability.

3. *Providing Training and Encouragement.* Perhaps there are no men in the church with sufficient ability to qualify as part-time music directors. In this case, a likely candidate should be chosen and encouraged to spend time with the music director of a neighboring church or to take a course in the local university or college in conducting and songleading.

Pastors who have taken conducting and song-leading in college can be of help to the man who has all the other qualifications but is lacking in musical training. A sincere Christian man, who desired to help his church, is personable and has a good platform appearance, and is willing to spend time learning to direct music, would make a good part-time music director.

He should be taught many things, among them, (a) to use the rhythm patterns in directing songs; (b) to announce the song numbers to the audience clearly and distinctly; (c) not to talk a great deal between stanzas or between songs; (d) how to sit on the platform, paying close attention during all the service; (e) how to direct the music for a large or small congregation (by this I mean he should be taught how to vary the size of the patterns that he uses, according to the size of the audience, and I will say more concerning this in the chapter on congregational singing and song leading); (f) to keep track of the songs used in each service so that he does not sing the same songs too often; (g) to follow the order of service correctly; (h) that the pastor is the leader of every service when present; (i) how to work with the accompanists; and (j) how to care for the musical instruments, making sure they are tuned periodically.

4. *Understanding of Policies and Duties.* Because many part-time music directors are part of the congregation prior to assuming their new duties, it is even more important that they understand the policies of the pastor and the church, and exactly what their duties will be, before taking the position. Many times a person who performs this task without charge to the church feels that he is entitled to a few liberties. It should be understood, in the beginning, that he is to follow the leadership of the pastor. This will prevent a great many problems in the future.

Counseling With the Music Director

1. *Frequency.* Because the music director and the pastor work so closely together in the services, the pastor should counsel with the music director frequently. The pastor should not give the music director specific orders, or make him feel that he has to discuss every little problem, but he should try to establish a good rapport between them, so that, whenever the need arises, they may confer.

The pastor and the music director should get to know each

other, perhaps on a little more intimate basis than the pastor and other staff members.

2. *Place.* The pastor's counseling should be done largely in private, whether in his office or in the music director's office. In any situation, no matter how close the pastor and his music director are in their personal lives, when each puts himself completely into his work, they will not see eye to eye in every situation. The pastor, a leader of the church, at times will have to disagree with certain actions or policies of the music director. His disagreement should always be kept on the highest Christian plane, and be expressed in private.

Occasionally, there might be a need for the pastor to reprimand the music director; this also should be done in private. Public reprimands are most embarrassing and actually cause the congregation to sympathize with the music director or other persons being reprimanded, and to oppose the pastor, or the reprimander. Therefore, the wise pastor will do his correcting in private. This will cause the music director to be more appreciative of him, and will draw them together.

3. *Subject of Discussions.* The music director and pastor should discuss many aspects of the church work, but some are so important they should have priority. They should discuss the order of service, problems that occasionally arise in the service, how to properly sing the invitation song, and changes to be made from time to time in the services. At times the music director and the pastor should evaluate the music program, to see if it is supplying the musical needs of the church.

The Pastor of the Music Program

Every pastor should be the head or the pastor of every phase of the church program: the board of deacons, the board of trustees, the finances of the church, the youth program, the Sunday school, the missionary society, the Training Union, and the choir program. And because he is the pastor of the music program, there are certain duties to be performed by him and certain considerations given to him.

He Determines the Direction of the
Music Program

As stated earlier, the pastor should be acutely aware of the needs of his people, not only in Bible teaching or preaching, but in the music program also. Every pastor should insist that the church have the kind of music program that he feels best for them.

He Guides in the Choosing of the Hymns

In each hymnal there are many songs not particularly good as congregational hymns. A relatively untrained part-time music director may not recognize exactly which hymns would make good congregational songs and which would not. Many times, too, the music director may differ with the pastor as to what type hymn should be sung in the services. The pastor should have some method of choosing what type hymns the congregation should sing. He could take the church hymnal and very carefully go through it, page by page, and mark the hymns he thinks best for the people to sing. He should give this book to the music director, asking him to choose songs from the ones marked. Of course, new songs can be added from time to time, and there are ways to do this, but time and space do not permit it in this chapter.

He Oversees Content and Preparation

Every music director will have a tendency to veer a little to the right or the left of the preference indicated by the pastor; therefore, it is up to the pastor to keep a close eye on the music program to make sure that the content is all that it should be at all times. He should also notice whether or not the music seems to be well prepared. This is one area in which he can be of great help to the music director, encouraging him to make sure that every number is ready for performance before going into a service.

He Approves Special Singers

Every special singer that goes on the platform should be approved by the pastor. This is important for several reasons. First of all, the pastor would come nearer knowing the lives of the church members than would the music director. Because every person who sings on the platform—in a special group or as a soloist—should be exemplary in his Christian life, the pastor should determine who will or will not sing. This is for the protection of the services as well as for the music director. Any criticism that might come to the music director because of some special singer that he has chosen is then referred to the pastor.

He Determines the Order of the Service

The pastor should determine when the congregation sings, when the Scriptures are read, when the offering is taken, and so on. He may make up the order of service and give a copy of it to the music director, who will then furnish a copy each week to everyone on the platform. But the original order should be determined by the pastor. This order of service could be followed each week. This is not to say that the pastor should not consult with the music director or other members of the staff in determining the order of service.

He Helps Promote the Music Program

Just as no other phase of the church program can be successful without active promotion by the pastor, the music program is destined to failure without his active promotion.

People will not join the choirs, as they ought to unless they feel that the pastor is one hundred per cent in favor of the choir program. The pastor ought occasionally to talk to the congregation about the need for a good choir—their need to give their talents to the Lord and to serve Him in this way. The pastor should occasionally compliment the choir and the fine job done by the music director. Most pastors desire to do this. This encourages the choir and helps them to know that the pastor is pleased. It makes for a much better spirit between the pastor and the music director. Many times the difference between success and failure in the building of a good choir program would be the promotion, or lack of promotion, of the choir program by the pastor.

Musical events such as the Christmas cantata or the Easter musical program should be promoted from the pulpit by the pastor. These events will be very lightly attended if the people are not sure that the pastor is in favor of the program or that he intends to be present himself and expects them to be.

In summary, every pastor ought to become the "pastor" of the music program of his church. Pastors should keep a close eye on the music program, help the music director in the promotion, encourage him, counsel with him, and be a definite part of this phase of the work God has called them to do.

Chapter XIX

The Music Director

Every part-time or full-time music director should feel definitely that he is in God's will in his present place of service. Few people in the church have as important a position as does the music director, other than the pastor. Because his position requires him to have such a large part in the public services, he should be God's choice for that particular job in the church which he serves.

Many people have the mistaken idea that a music director waves his arms on Sunday morning, leads the congregational singing, leads the choir, is in charge of a few specials, and his week's work is over. Nothing could be further from the truth concerning the kind of music director every church should have. The short time spent in the Sunday services is only the showcase of many hours of work done during the week. All that a music director is and does comes together at this particular time. This is the time for which he has prepared all week. Whether he succeeds or fails depends upon the singers and musicians and his work through the week.

As has been stated earlier in this book, nothing is more needful in churches today than God-called music directors. God needs men who are willing to give of themselves in this important task.

A Full-time or Part-time Music Director

Many churches cannot afford to hire a full-time music director. This does not in any way relieve the part-time or "volunteer" music director from being all that he should be, in the sight of God and of the church that he serves. The attitudes, insight, and characteristics of the full-time music director ought to be embodied in a part-time music director.

More is expected of a full-time music director, because he is paid to give his time to this task. Most part-time music directors have other work to finance their living. Although music directors have other tasks that do not pertain to the music program— visitation, teaching Sunday school, youth work, and perhaps correlating religious education—their foremost task is to see that the church has the best music program possible.

When guests visit a home, the family members try to see that the room where the guests will be entertained is even more emaculately kept than other parts of the home. The public services are the "living rooms" of the church, where people come to enjoy the church. This is where they spend their time and where they should feel welcome. This is where they should see the church operating at its maximum efficiency.

Because this is true, the music director should be enthusiastic about having the kind of music program that will cause those without Christ to be led to knowledge of Him, partly because of an evangelistic music program.

Naturally the part-time music director is not expected to spend as much time as a full-time man but if he assumes the responsibility of the music program of his church, then he should see to it that his church has as good a music program as he can cause to come into being. Anything less than this, even from a part-time music director, is sinful in the sight of God.

Bear in mind, however, that God does not expect more than a man has. He does not expect one to give of talents he does not possess, but He does say, "It is required in stewards that a man be found faithful." Either a part-time or full-time music director should be sure to give his best.

Attitude

The attitude of the music director is of prime importance. Many talented music directors have had their programs curtailed by their bad attitudes. If the music director's attitude is unbecoming to a dedicated Christian, it would indicate that perhaps he is not in the position that God would have him in, or that his heart is not right toward the work God has given him to do.

The attitude of the music director should be right as concerns the following:

The Church Member

Every music director should keep in mind that he is to be a servant of the church. Too many music directors are willing and ready to receive with open arms the generosities of the church members, but they are not willing to reciprocate. Let it also be kept in mind that the church members pay the salary of the music director. They have the right to expect of him a certain amount of his time, energy, and effort.

Every music director should spend time in prayer, asking God to give him a good attitude toward the members of his church. This is very difficult in the face of criticism or shortsightedness on the part of people, but it is one of the difficult tasks of being a music director. A good attitude pays off in large dividends.

Music directors should learn to love people; people will return his love.

The Music Program

The music program is the task to which God has called the music director and should receive his primary attention. He should determine that, under God, he will develop the best possible music program for his church. Many directors could have a much better music program if they spent a little more time and effort in consciously trying to make it the best possible.

No aspect of the music program is of little importance. Anything worth doing at all is worth doing well. If a music director trains a quartet, then it should be the best quartet that can be developed in the church. Every aspect of the program should strive to be the best part of the music program.

Thousands of people have been attracted to a particular church because of an excellent music program; therefore, no part of the work of any church should surpass her music program.

The Pastor

Above all, the music director should realize that the thirteenth chapter of Hebrews applies to him also. Any time God chose to lead a group of people he did so by using one man. God usually spoke to this individual, and he to the people. The same is true today. When God leads a church to become a great lighthouse—a great soul-winning station—he uses an individual. The pastor should oversee the whole church; the music director must recognize him as overseer. He may not always agree with the pastor, but his wishes and desires must be subordinate to the wishes and desires of the pastor.

Many people consider the music director as "second fiddle" to the pastor. Humanly speaking, this is true in every sense of the word. Although God does not have any second, third, fourth, or first fiddles, every man who does the will of God and tries his best to please Him, plays first fiddle as far as God is concerned.

Blessed is the music director who keeps in focus his position in respect to the pastor. Never should a day go by but that the music director prays for the pastor, asking God to direct him in every activity. He should feel free to communicate with the pastor on any subject, and should provide the pastor with plenty of time to counsel with him.

His good attitude toward the pastor in everyday life, all week long, will make for a good attitude on the platform during the public services.

His Helpers

No music director can carry on a full music program without help from other people; therefore, his attitude toward those who help him should be one of kindness and appreciation. Perhaps he knows more about the music program or about music in general than they do, but his appreciative attitude toward them will cause them to do a much better job, even in their limited capacity. Never should he give the impression (in any way) that he is better than they; that attitude would only ostracize him.

Choir Members

A music director's attitude should be the finest toward the members of his choirs. His choirs are made up of individuals who have feelings and personalities that must be considered. Each person likes to have a certain amount of credit when a performance has been particularly good. Each wants to be recognized by the director for what he is and who he is.

If a music director can establish good rapport between himself and his choir members, then 90 per cent of his battles are over. The music will be sweeter, the attitude of the choir will be better, and the services will benefit from the closeness of the music director and choir member.

The director should lead the choir members to understand that his position carries with it a certain authority in rehearsals and in the music activities under his direction. He must, at all times, command the respect of those who sing under him. This he can do only if they see that he means business and attempts to be fair with them in all things. They must know first, though, that he loves them.

The Accompanists

The pianist and the organist can do much to make a music director look good. It has almost become my conviction that no music program can far exceed the ability of the accompanists. There are ways to compensate for the lack of ability on the part of the accompanists. When possible, it should be done; but, as a general rule the music chain cannot be stronger than this particular link.

Just as the pastor and the music director should have a good attitude toward each other, the music director and the accompanists should have a good working relationship, mainly because they work so closely together in the public services. Never be mistaken about this fact: the audience can tell when there is enmity between the music director and his accompanists. Such attitudes grieve the Holy Spirit and will, in many cases, hinder the public services.

Here again, the music director must let it be known that he is in charge and has responsibilities and authority under the general leadership of the pastor. Once the accompanists understand this, a certain amount of rapport is built up automatically. Every music director should strive for as good a working relationship as possible between himself and the accompanists.

Training

While every full-time music director is expected to have adequate training for his position, many part-time music directors have had little or no formal training. The full-time music director should never be content with past successes; he should be always looking for new ideas and new ways of developing his music program. His training or learning should never end; when it does, his effectiveness ends.

It is good for a music director to attend summer music camps or seminars. Several good seminars are held each year throughout the United States. Many churches will pay the expenses of their music directors to these. Just as a doctor needs to keep abreast of the changing practices in the medical world, a music director needs to keep abreast of new developments, new music, and new techniques. It is easy for music directors to slip into complacency, while their methods could be greatly improved and augmented by a week in a good music seminar, getting new ideas for conducting and directing.

The part-time music director should also take every opportunity to learn to do his job better. If he is near a college or university (preferably a Christian college), he should audit classes in conducting, song leading, and music theory. If he is not paid by the church, the church should bear the expense of his classroom activities. If this is not possible, he should contact a full-time music director in whom he has confidence, and seek advice and counsel. Usually, a full-time music director with formal training, whose aid is sought by one who wants to become a better part-time music director, will help in every way possible.

Weekly sessions should be arranged for the trained musician to teach the untrained how to direct a choir, to lead the congregational singing, to announce the numbers, to recruit new choir members, and to develop small groups and ensembles.

Every pastor who has a part-time music director should see to it that he has some kind of training to qualify him to direct the music of the church. The pastor can help by teaching him how to sit on the platform, how to announce the numbers, what to say and what not to say between numbers, and how to approach the pulpit. Hundreds of services have been ruined because a pastor did not have the foresight or take the time to go over a few details with the untrained music director, to make the services more enjoyable.

It is not a disgrace for a church to have a part-time music director with no training, but this situation should not continue without effort toward improvement.

Insight

Every music director should realize that God has given him a job to do, and should look for ways to do it better. He should ask God to give him more ability to meet the real spiritual needs of the people, through the music program. He should make notes often when confronted with a situation over which he has no control so that he might improve the situation should it occur at a later time.

Soul Winning

Any music director can do a much better job on Sunday if he has spent some time during the week in witnessing, trying to win people to Jesus Christ. He should have a fire burning within his heart on Sunday during the services, and there is no better way to kindle it than through soul winning. This will cause the services to be more enjoyable to him, and will cause him to do a better job.

The music director should set a definite time each week to go soul winning; if this is not done, he usually will not go as he should. A soul-winning music director communicates his feelings and the burden on his heart more effectively. Just as the pastor, the Sunday school teachers, the associate pastors and others of the church are expected to win souls and to witness for Jesus Christ, it is the director's duty to do the same.

Personal Characteristics

A music director should be honest, upright, amiable, loving, kind, happy, respectful, cheerful, and determined. He should not necessarily possess all these qualities at one and the same time, but they should be, eventually, a part of his makeup. These are positive aspects.

Now consider a few negative ones. May God have mercy on a *lazy* music director. Many good directors receive a certain amount of reproach because of lazy predecessors. There is no place in the field of music for a lazy person. A music director should check the list and see if he has the desirable characteristics and leaves off the undesirable characteristics as possible.

Charisma

The word "charisma" has come to mean something altogether

different from what is here intended. No reference to the Pentecostal use of the term is meant, but rather the leadership ability of the music director to relate to the audience and to instill within them a desire to sing and participate in the service, following his directions.

Every director does not have this innately, but should strive for a better director-audience relationship. Often different geographical locations affect this, but a wise director will have character enough to say to himself, "I'll do whatever is necessary, short of compromising my convictions, to lead these people in the way that will honor Christ." A good audience-director relationship is sometimes long in coming but the sweetness of the accomplishment always mellows the experience in reaching the desired goal.

One of the best ways for an aspiring young music director to develop charisma with an audience is to watch carefully some outstanding directors, noting procedures, mannerisms and methods they use in "reaching" an audience. He should not become a carbon copy, but he should try to gain from these directors some tips to help him improve. Then, too, on occasion, he can learn how not to reach an audience by carefully observing a music director lose contact with the people.

Cultivating leadership ability is another effort to reach people with the Gospel of Jesus Christ. Many would say that the Holy Spirit can override human failures and weaknesses, but God gives us knowledge and ability and expects us to be "as wise as serpents and harmless as doves." He expects us to "pray as if everything depended on Him and work as if everything depended on us." He expects us to approach every service as though it were our last one and to strive with everything that is in us to reach every last person in the audience. Sometimes it is only done through the music and the music director.

In summary, a music director, full-time or part-time, should make sure that he is the best music director that he can be. Make sure that his attitudes, training, insight, soul winning, and personal characteristics are all that they can be under God.

Chapter XX

Helpful Hints for the Music Director

Consider at this point twelve "do's" and twelve "don'ts" for a good music director. In order to end on a positive note, let's take the don'ts first.

1. Don't neglect preparation. The choir can immediately sense when the conductor is ill-prepared for the choir practice.

2. Don't organize the complete music program all at one time.

3. Don't lead the people faster than they are willing and able to follow. Give them time to digest what you have already given them.

4. Don't criticize the music director who preceded you.

5. Don't make too many sudden changes.

6. Don't organize all the choirs at once. Start with the adult choir and get it to rolling smoothly. Then move quickly on to the teenage choir, the Junior choir, and the children's choirs.

7. Don't let criticism discourage you.

8. Don't let your personal ideas and tastes dominate the complete music program. Consider the likes and dislikes of others in your planning of the music.

9. Don't overlook the other departments of the church work. Realize that the people who are involved in the music program are also involved in other areas of the church work, and they must give some time to other responsibilities. Try not to cause their loyalties to be divided or force them to choose between two positions in which they are serving Christ.

10. Don't forget that you are working with all kinds of people.

11. Don't allow your time to be used by too many duties outside the church.

12. Don't lose the spirit of humility.

Now here are twelve do's for a good choir director.

1. Always be sincere about your work.
2. Develop confidence in yourself.
3. Be friendly to everyone.
4. Develop vitality.
5. Develop a good music ear. Many times a music director has to really work at this. This does not come naturally for some people.
6. Display real joy in directing the choirs.
7. Be flexible at all times. Try to come to the place where you can make changes smoothly in the middle of a service.
8. Learn to mold an audience, encouraging their participation in the music program of the service, thereby preparing them for the pastor's message to follow.
9. Have a sense of humor. Be able to laugh at yourself.
10. Be ever learning.
11. Keep a good Christian testimony.
12. By all means, be a soul winner.

Here are several other tips that will prove helpful to music directors in most situations.

1. Make sure the pianist and the organist can see all of the platform, so they can watch every move that the director makes, and make sure they do watch.
2. The first word of the choir number is most important. If the first word is strong and full of assurance, the audience relaxes. They sense that you know exactly what you are doing, that you have practiced well, and they will enjoy and be blessed by the choir number.
3. Don't call attention to mistakes or difficult passages. If a person in the choir makes a mistake, just pretend for the moment that it didn't happen. Ask the choir members not to nudge each other, or to call attention to themselves during difficult passages by frowning or shaking the head.
4. Ask the choir not to chew gum or talk, distracting the audience.

5. Ask choir members to be careful of bored or concerned expressions. Many times the attitude of the audience is set by the facial expressions of those in the choir. Tell them to "enjoy the services and make sure it shows on your face."

6. Have the choir open the services. It seems that every service can be started a little better with a vibrant opening choir number. It should be a short, special arrangement of a chorus or the refrain of a gospel song or hymn.

7. Always have a good ending on every choir special. If there is a good beginning and a good ending, the audience seems to forget most of what went on in between. To be sure of an effective ending, spend a great deal of time practicing it.

8. Have the choir rehearse at least one verse of the congregational numbers for the following Sunday at each rehearsal. This does two things: (1) It allows them to better lead the congregational singing; (2) It helps them to warm up and get ready for the practice of the special choir arrangements.

9. Urge the choir always to sit and stand erect. Nothing looks more slouchy or careless than choir members sitting on the tip of their spine or standing in a leaning position. Besides giving a poor appearance, they cannot sing or perform well in such a position.

10. Teach the choir to sing in a relaxed manner, with the mouth open wide vertically, to produce better tone quality. It softens and mellows the harsh tones.

11. Choose good rehearsal times, when most of the members can be present. Sometimes it is better to rehearse after the Wednesday night service; sometimes it is better on a special night.

The Adult choir at First Baptist Church of Hammond practices from 7:00 to 8:30 on Thursday evening, and from 6:15 to 6:45 on Sunday evenings. The Teenage-choir rehearsal is from 5:00 to 6:00 on Sunday afternoon. The Junior, Primary, and Beginner choirs practice from 6:30 to 7:15 on Wednesday evening, during the teachers and officers meeting.

12. Always try to vary the program a little bit; make sure it is vibrant, alive, and evangelistic. When people hear your choirs

sing, they should sense that they believe what they are singing. This can only be true with an evangelistic music program. Anthems and classical sacred music are good; but be sure that everything in the service leads to soul winning, warmth, and Christian love.

Chapter XXI

Christian Music in the Home

No place in the world should be happier than our homes. Where there is happiness, there is always singing; therefore, a great deal of singing is done in a happy home, perhaps more in some than in others, but always singing. Fortunate indeed are children born to parents who enjoy singing and are musically inclined. This does not mean that parents who are not musical cannot recognize the need for music and provide music opportunities for their children.

There are many aspects of music in the home but the music to be discussed in this chapter is the music learned at church and carried over into the home, and the music learned at home and carried into the church. There are many ways that music can be a great asset to the home.

Many men, in their later years, are reminded of their childhood training in the home at a mother's knee, through hearing a song that brought back golden memories. Singing indelibly imprints the blessings of God and Christian doctrines in the minds of young children. Many children first exhibit a knowledge of Christian teachings through the songs learned in the Sunday school classes. Children bring songs into the home, and the songs are shared in the happy home situations.

The singing or home musical participation need not even be of high caliber from a musical standpoint, but it can be an effective tool in the hands of Christian parents.

TOTAL PARTICIPATION

Whether in the family altar or in other home situations, all the family should be encouraged to participate in the music in the home. Each child should share equally in musical training opportunities; if music lessons are extended to one, they should be given to all who are old enough. Older children who did not have the opportunity for music training may encourage younger brothers and sisters to take advantage of present opportunities. Every member of the family should be exposed to Christian music, whether in family songfest, music lessons, sacred recordings, or attendance at musical concerts.

Family singing can be carried on at various times when all can naturally and freely sing together.

At Devotions

After Scripture reading and prayer, all the family may sing together a hymn or a chorus that one of the children has learned and loves. To link a Christian doctrine to a melody is to cement it in the mind, because one can go about humming the tune while the words play through the mind. He is thus repeating the lessons learned in the family togetherness times.

Good Morning, Lord: Family Devotions From Famous Hymns is a book of family devotions I have written. It suggests that, after the Scripture passage is read and a favorite verse memorized, the story behind a famous Christian song be used as a devotional thought.

After this lesson is learned and the hymn history tucked away into the minds, the family may sing the song around the family altar. After this, a devotional thought may close the period. Use of Christian songs and choruses in your home during the devotional period is highly recommended.

On Automobile Trips

Some of my family's most delightful times were spent riding along, singing wonderful gospel songs and choruses, including those the children were learning in Sunday school. As these were repeated again and again, they joined the growing list of songs that our family knows. Over the miles another and another was learned, until the family can sing a great many songs together.

Some fathers and mothers say, "I can't carry a tune in a bucket." They should forget that bit of nonsense and join the songs, even though they may sing every note on the same pitch. The idea is to enter into the joy and spirit of the occasion, not to become a part of a great musical production.

At Family Get-Togethers or Reunions

Nothing seems to please grandparents quite so much as the singing of their grandchildren. Therefore, the children should be encouraged to join in a little songfest while visiting Grandma and Grandpa. The time spent around the piano singing the songs of the church will be golden memories in years to come. This is not always possible, but whenever possible such singing should be engaged in with joy.

Music Lessons

Many families are so hard-pressed financially that it is almost impossible for their children to take private music lessons. Today with the great advancement in music study in public and private schools, many children, who could not otherwise afford it, may be able to have some music instruction. Parents should make sure that their children take advantage of every opportunity, so they can serve Christ well when they grow into young men and women. If the school furnishes instruments and free lessons, these should be utilized.

Pianos and other musical instruments are very costly, and some cannot afford them. Those who can should encourage their children to appreciate the opportunity of music lessons and to apply themselves to practice.

Young children who learn the basic piano keyboard are headed in the right direction for serious music training, because all music stems from the concert key, which is the piano keyboard. It would be greatly beneficial for young people who plan to study any type of instrument to know something about the piano keyboard. An ability to play the piano well yields many opportunities for Christian service.

Young, immature minds cannot see the end from the beginning and therefore are not capable of seeing the value of hours of rehearsal and diligent study. If children are forced to continue in what they have started, they will learn a lesson in perseverance. They need not continue indefinitely, but they should keep up their commitment to the project until they and the parents see that it is useless to continue or until real progress is achieved.

In a child's instrumental practice, time becomes a factor; school becomes a factor; the family schedule becomes a factor; many other things too numerous to mention enter into the picture. These difficulties need to be worked out, not because you are trying to train a great musician, but because you are trying to teach a child a lesson that will be valuable to him in life in many, many other situations.

HOW FAMILY MUSIC HELPS
THE CHURCH

While all the varied details of this subject cannot be discussed, we can say that, in a very real sense, the music programs in our churches would be but a fraction of their present size if it were not for music in the homes. This takes in private music lessons for some children, singing around the family altar and on automobile trips, family encouragement of children entering into school and church music activities, and the willingness of parents to finance family music projects.

Many of our Adult choirs are what they are, because years ago parents saw the need to train their children musically, and these children in turn have become adults and are in strategic places in the choir, leading those with less music training. Church music would be crippled if it were not for homes that encourage participation in music.

Chapter XXII

Effective Congregational Singing

By Dr. J. R. Faulkner

I am frank to state that, in my opinion, congregational singing would take the Number 2 place in the ministry of the Word, but it is essential to an effective ministry. It is true that congregational singing has a ministry within itself, because it conveys the great truths of the Word of God. It also has a therapeutic value for people. It quiets their minds and hearts and brings them into an attitude of worship, preparing them to receive the truth of God's Word as it is delivered by the minister later in the service. I do not think that the music should ever take the place of the preaching of the Word of God, but it should be a handmaiden to revival and to an effective Bible ministry.

Happy is the song leader who has a well-trained organist and pianist who pay attention to him as he opens the service. I have been blessed in this regard through all the years of my ministry at Highland Park Baptist Church. Our accompanists are quick to note the simple gesture that is the signal to begin. I may never look at the organist after bringing the people to their feet, but with a simple motion with my left hand signal for her to begin the accompaniment. I ask the accompanist to always play the first phrase of the song for an introduction. This brings to mind the words of the first verse and makes it easier for the people to begin with me. I never encourage a long introduction; just an opening measure or two is sufficient.

When announcing a song, I give the number first, and then I make a brief comment about the song or give a word of encouragement to the people to join with us as we sing. I always repeat the number of the song for those who are slow listeners and do not get it the first time. They will be thumbing through the index, so I repeat the number at the close of my comment.

There are certain unwritten rules that I follow in selecting songs and hymns for the service. I begin with one that is well known and very singable. If I plan to use a hymn that is lesser known, I present it as the second or third song in the format. I try to follow the theme established by the pastor in his message, if possible. If not, I concentrate on instilling the proper attitude into the people so that they are ready for the message, whatever it might be. Since our pastor is a musician and loves for people to sing vigorously, I choose at least one song in our evening service that leads to a dramatic ending. Notable examples are "One Day" and "Heaven Came Down and Glory Filled My Soul." There are many others in our better hymnals. If I am bringing the service to a prayer time, I try to use songs with a stilling effect to induce a more worshipful spirit. I give the service to the pastor in a lowered tone. On the other hand, if announcements or offering are next, I end my part of the song service on a high, inspirational tone.

In choosing songs I try to remember the key signatures as well as the time signatures. I think this adds to variety in the service and makes for more enthusiastic singing.

The size of the conducting pattern is regulated by the size of the audience. At the Highland Park Baptist Church I'm leading 2,000 to 3,500 people in an average congregation, and, naturally, I work with arms at full length. I use a smaller pattern with smaller congregations.

I avoid repeating ordinary songs within a thirty-day period. I keep a record of every song used and how many times it has been used in our services; even the use of gospel choruses. I can check with my secretary to find out how many times we have used any song within the past six to twelve months. I have an old hymnal that I use to prepare my song services. I make a pencil notation in the margin of the book as to when I last used each song. I even keep a notation of the songs used by visiting musicians.

I do not dominate the pulpit until my pastor is present. For instance, in opening the morning service, for years I did not sit down on the platform until my pastor put in his appearance. If I chose to sit down, I sat in one of the chairs by the piano or organ and waited until my pastor approached. Prior to this, I would have checked the PA system, the organ, and all the electronic equipment we use. I would check the building for lights or for any problems relating to the ushering. These things are checked thirty to forty-five minutes before every regular service. If I have the responsibility of being in the pulpit prior to my pastor's appearance—and occasionally I do—when he appears I immediately stand and wait until he is seated. Our choir is then brought in at the given time with an organ accompaniment. They remain standing till all are in position. We have the opening number by the choir, and then I turn to the audience to begin the congregational singing.

(Dr. J. R. Faulkner, writer of this chapter, was co-pastor of Highland Park Baptist Church in Chattanooga, Tennessee, and led the congregational singing of that great church for many years.)